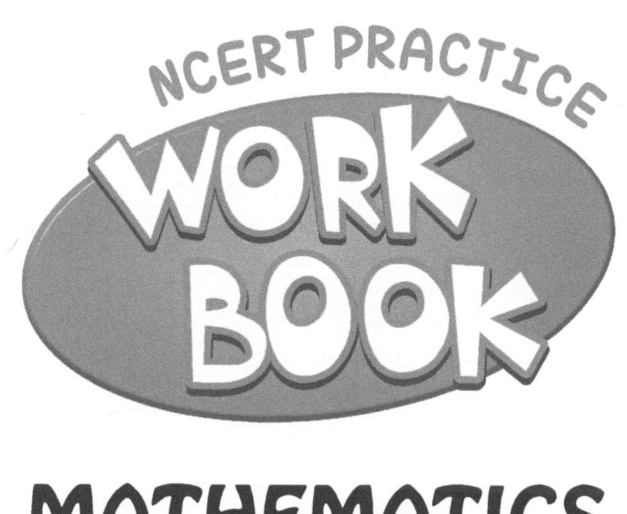

MATHEMATICS

MATHEMATICS

MATH-MAGIC

Rashmi Jaiswal

ARIHANT PRAKASHAN, MEERUT

WORKBOOK MATHEMATICS 5th

Published by Arihant Prakashan, Meerut

Administrative & Production Offices

Regd. Office
'Ramchhaya' 4577/15, Agarwal Road, Darya Ganj, New Delhi -110002
Tele: 011- 47630600, 43518550; Fax: 011- 23280316

Head Office
Kalindi, TP Nagar, Meerut (UP) - 250002
Tel: 0121-2401479, 2512970, 4004199; Fax: 0121-2401648

Sales & Support Offices
Agra, Ahmedabad, Bengaluru, Bhubaneswar, Bareilly, Chennai, Delhi, Guwahati, Hyderabad, Jaipur, Jhansi, Kolkata, Lucknow, Meerut, Nagpur & Pune.

ISBN 978-93-11121-94-9

Price ₹ 80.00

Production Team
Publishing Manager
Keshav Mohan, Amit Verma
Project Head
Karishma Yadav
Project Coordinator
Pooja Chaudhary
Project Editor
Priya Mittal
Cover Designer
Shanu Mansoori
Inner Designer
Ravi Negi
DTP Operators
Ravi Sagar, Kamal
Proof Readers
Tarun Sharma

For further information about the products from Arihant, log on to www.arihantbooks.com or e-mail to info@arihantbooks.com

Workbook, Why?

"Knowledge will not be with you for Long Unless You Practice"

This quotation answer the above question 'Workbook, Why?' perfectly, i.e Workbooks are made to give the students practice required to achieve perfection & mastery in the subject. These are the only Workbooks, which are strictly based on **NCERT, the only recommended books by Govt. of India & CBSE** (reference Circular No. Acad-41/2015 dated 20th July 2015).

Given below is the detailed description of Workbook and some of its special features

ONLY WORKBOOK BASED ON NCERT

NCERT textbooks are the only textbooks, which have been prepared according to National Curriculum Framework, which discourages the idea of rote learning rather they focus on understanding and try to make the students able to identify the way of problem solving.

Keeping the importance of NCERT textbooks in mind we have prepared this Workbook, strictly based on NCERT content, this Workbook will complement NCERT by providing practice on the material given in each chapter of NCERT textbook, making the students understand the chapter completely.

WORKBOOK- PURPOSE, USE & FEATURES

This Workbook, through its **numerous exercises** having different **variety of questions** covering each and every fact of NCERT, will prove to be **equally useful** for both, **Classroom** and at **Home**. One more purpose of this Workbook is to provide the students a **systematic practice** of the content taught in the class and what they study in the textbooks.

Some special features of this workbook are

- Complete Coverage of each chapter for complete practice
- Different variety of questions; Fill in the Blanks, True-False, Matching, Multiple Choice Questions, Differentiate between, Define the following, One word for, Odd One Out, Very Short Answer, Short Answer, Long Answer Type etc.
- Many Questions given in each chapter are related with day-to-day activities making them interesting to solve.
- Keeps the students actively engaged with the content and develop enquiry skills.

WORKBOOK-DESIGNED TO IMPROVE SUBJECT ABILITIES

All the material given in this workbook is tailored to suit subject content with equal support on learning, which will surely help students to boost their abilities and confidence in the subject.

We look forward for the feedback from students, teachers and parents for the further improvement of the contents of this book. We will try to update the contents according to your feedback in further editions of this Workbook.

The Publisher

Contents

[Chapter 1]

The Fish Tale

1 Given below are the dimensions of a whale shark and a fish. Count the number of fishes required to complete the length of whale shark and fill in the blanks. One has been done for you.

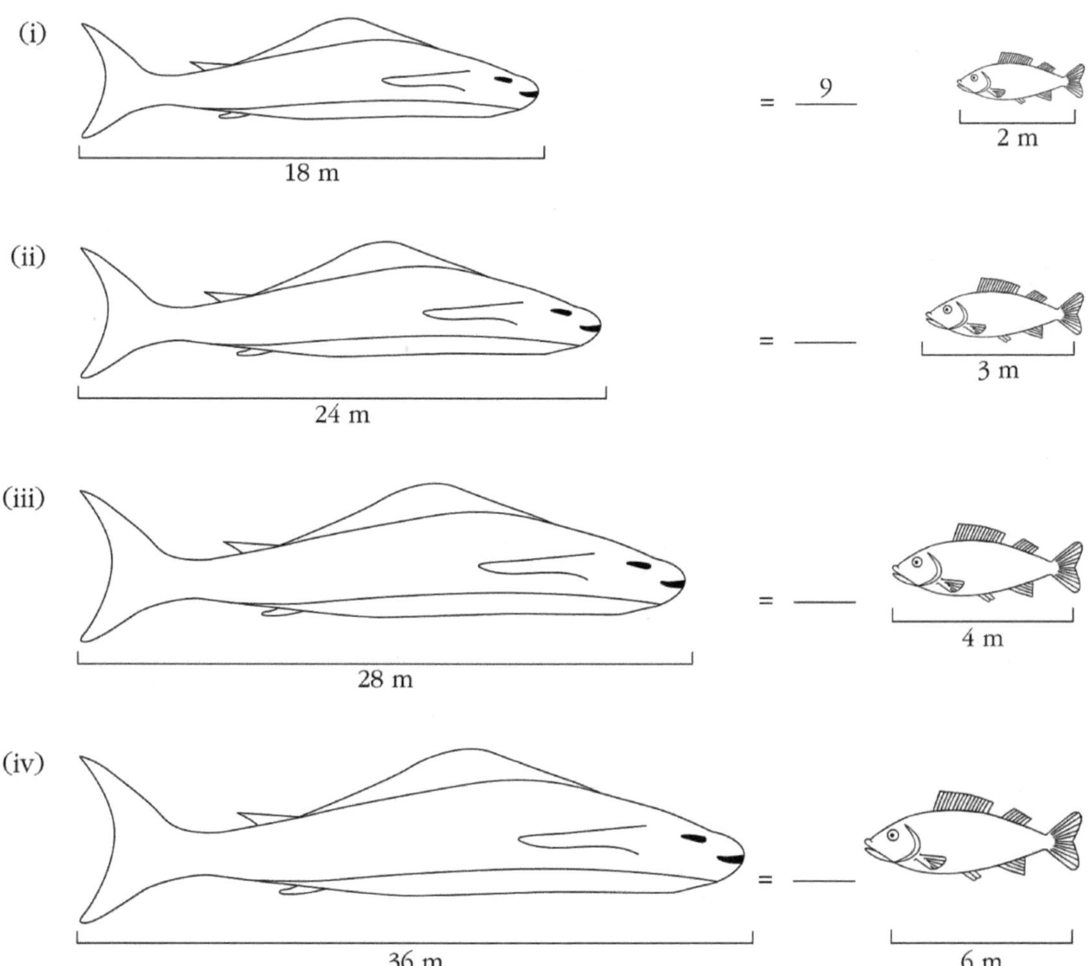

2 Solve the following and estimate the sum to nearest hundred.

(i)
$$\begin{array}{r} 78945 \\ +\ 30108 \\ \hline \end{array}$$

Estimated sum = ______

(ii)
$$\begin{array}{r} 68294 \\ +\ 21374 \\ \hline \end{array}$$

Estimated sum = ______

(iii)
$$\begin{array}{r} 14425 \\ +\ 12061 \\ \hline \end{array}$$

Estimated sum = ______

(iv)
$$\begin{array}{r} 6988 \\ -\ 5785 \\ \hline \end{array}$$

Estimated sum = ______

(v)
$$\begin{array}{r} 9875 \\ -\ 8596 \\ \hline \end{array}$$

Estimated sum = ______

(vi)
$$\begin{array}{r} 342 \\ \times\ 2 \\ \hline \end{array}$$

Estimated sum = ______

3 Find the difference between the given numbers and estimate the difference to nearest thousand. One has been done for you

(i) 68957 and 59874 = 9083 Estimated difference = 9000

(ii) 640140 and 411245 = ______ Estimated difference = ______

(iii) 142254 and 80618 = ______ Estimated difference = ______

(iv) (93216 + 7814) and 36245 = ______ Estimated difference = ______

4 Study the given table and answer the questions asked below.

Boat type	Distance covered in one trip (in km)	Time to cover distance in one trip (in hours)	Number of fishes caught in one trip
Long boat	20	4	20
Long tail boat	48	4	500
Motor boat	30	1	600
Machine boat	44	2	4000

(i) If long tail boat has to travel 72 km, how long it will take? How many fishes it can catch?

____

(ii) How many fishes can a motor boat catch in 5 h?

____

(iii) Find the difference between the number of fishes caught by motor boat and long tail boat in a time span of 6 h.

____

(iv) Machine boat caught 20000 fish. How long it must have travelled?

____

5 Fill in the blanks. One has been done for you

(i) ___1___ lakh = 1 hundred thousand

(ii) 100 lakh = ________ crore.

(iii) ________ is the same as ten thousand hundred.

(iv) ________ should be added to 99000 to get one lakh.

(v) ________ zeroes are there in one lakh.

(vi) Half of two lakh = ________ lakh.

6 State 'True' or 'False'.

	True/False
(i) 10000 is the greatest five-digit number.	________
(ii) In a lakh, there are hundred thousand.	________
(iii) Cost of 1 kg rice is ₹ 40. In ₹ 1000, a person can buy 20 kg rice.	________
(iv) 10 lakh = ten thousand hundred	________

7 There are different types of fish in a fish shop. The rates of all fish are given below

Fish type	Rate
Eel	₹ 50/kg
Red Snapper	₹ 80/kg
Parrot fish	₹ 50/kg
Dry fish	₹ 25/kg

(i) Yashi went to market to buy different fishes whose weight is shown in the below table. Initially, she had ₹ 1000 with her and after buying the three types of fishes, she bought some dry fish from the remaining money. How much dry fish did she buy?

Fish type	**Weight (bought)**
Eel	3 kg
Red Snapper	5 kg
Parrot fish	4 kg
Dry fish	—

(ii) Maya has ₹ 200. She spends one-fourth of the money on buying Eel and another three-fourth on buying dry fish.

(a) How many kilograms of Eel did she buy?

(b) How many kilograms of Dry fish did she buy?

(iii) When a fresh fish is dried, it becomes 1/3 of its weight. If Rahul spent ₹ 6000 to buy Eel fish and then dry it, then how many kilograms of dried Eel fish will be left with him?

8 The distance between Patna and Delhi is 1000 km. Raju wants to go to Patna from Delhi. He catches the train at 4 : 30 pm. Speed of the train is 100 km/h. At what time will he be able to reach Patna?

9 The owner of an orchard kept records of how many apples were picked in the past 5 days as shown in the table below. On which day was the most apples picked? What is the difference between the maximum and minimum number of apples picked on a particular day?

Day	Number of apples
Sunday	4319
Monday	4314
Thursday	4931
Wednesday	3492
Friday	2943

10 Rajesh took a loan of ₹ 9850 from the bank. He paid back ₹ 12240 to the bank in one year giving equal amount in each month. How much interest did he return? How much did he pay back every month?

11 In a school, there are ten classes. Each class has four sections and each section has equal number of students. If altogether there are 1600 students in the school, then how many students are there in each section of a class?

12 In a village, a Cooperative Bank was set up with the help of villagers. There were 2500 active members in the bank and the capital of bank was contributed by its members. Each member contributed equally. The total capital of the bank at the time of opening was ₹ 175000. Find the contribution of each member.

[Chapter 2]

Shapes and Angles

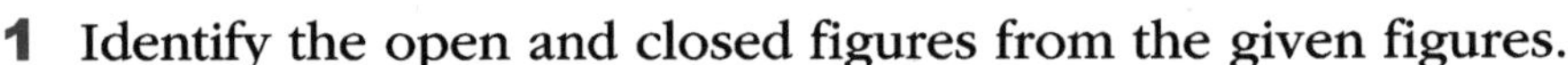

1 Identify the open and closed figures from the given figures.

(i) 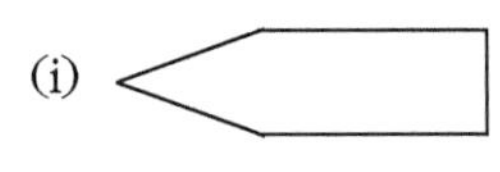 (ii)  (iii) 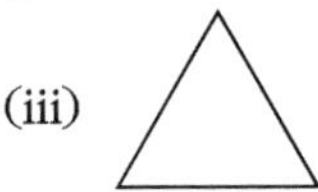

(iv) 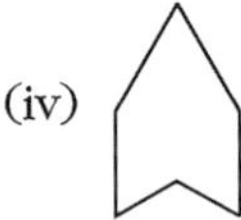 (v) 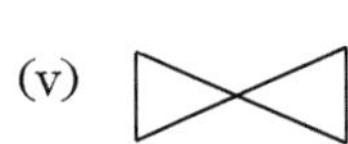 (vi) 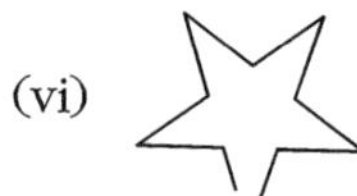

2 Fill in the blanks and write the number of matchsticks used to make the given figure. One has been done for you.

	Shape	Number of matchsticks
(i)	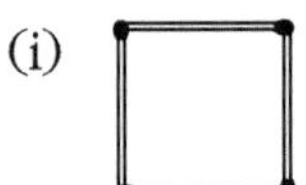	4
(ii)		____________
(iii)	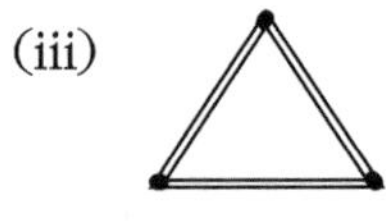	____________
(iv)	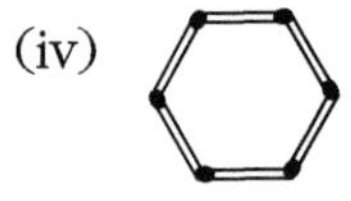	____________
(v)	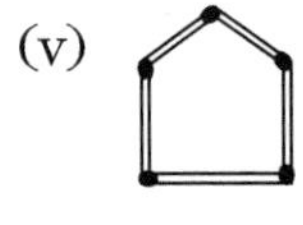	____________
(vi)	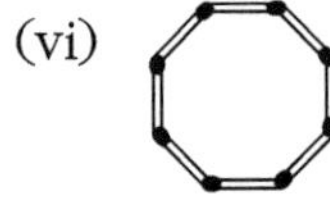	____________

3 Four different angles are marked in the below shapes. Identify the marked angles as acute angle, obtuse angle or right angle.

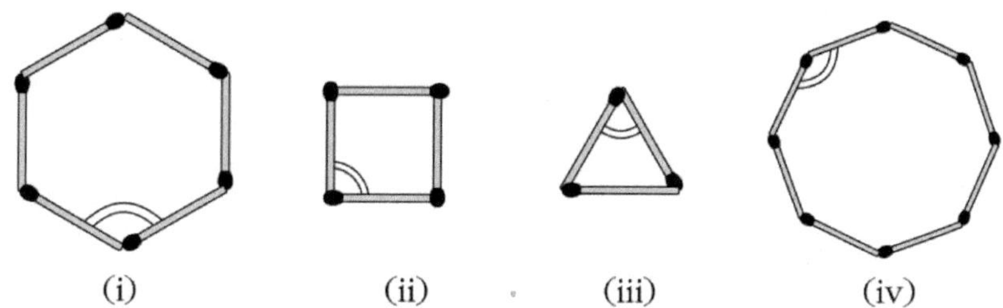

(i) (ii) (iii) (iv)

4 Match them correctly.

	Column A		**Column B**
(i)		(a)	Straight angle
(ii)	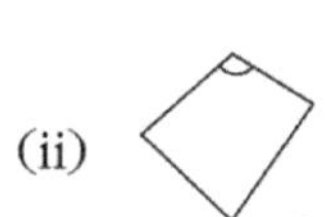	(b)	Right angle
(iii)	12, 9, 3, 6	(c)	Acute angle
(iv)		(d)	Obtuse angle

5 Identify the angles as right angle, acute angle, obtuse angle or straight angle. One has been done for you.

(i) 45° = acute angle (ii) 75° = ________

(iii) 165° = ________ (iv) 90° = ________

(v) 180° = ________ (vi) 35° = ________

6 Observe the following figure and answer the given questions.

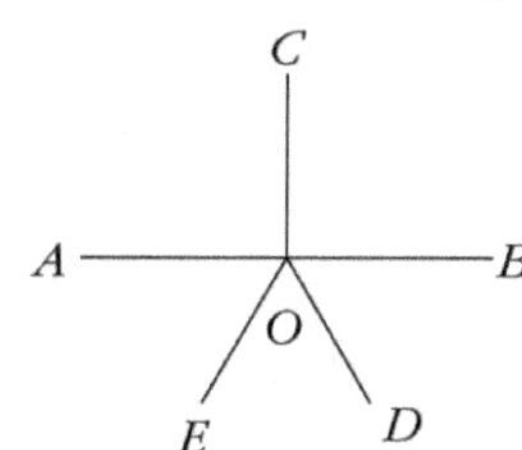

(i) Name the common vertex.

(ii) Name the right angles.

(iii) Name the acute angles.

(iv) Name the obtuse angles.

7 Count the number of angles in the given figures and write them in the space provided.

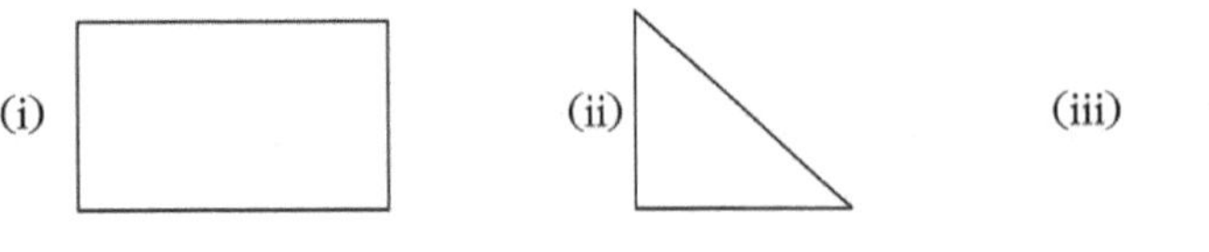

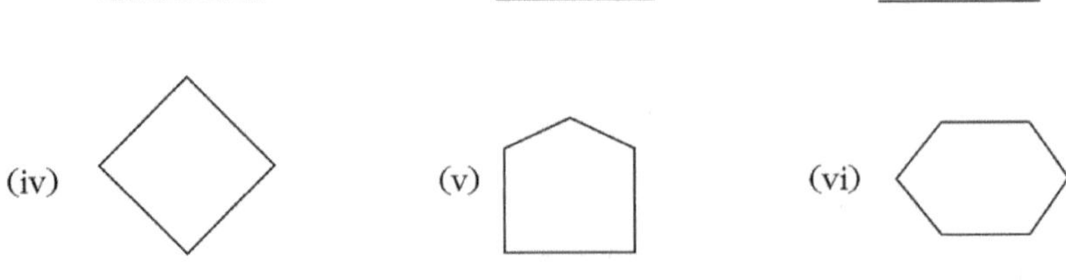

8 Write the type of angles made by the hands of the following clocks.

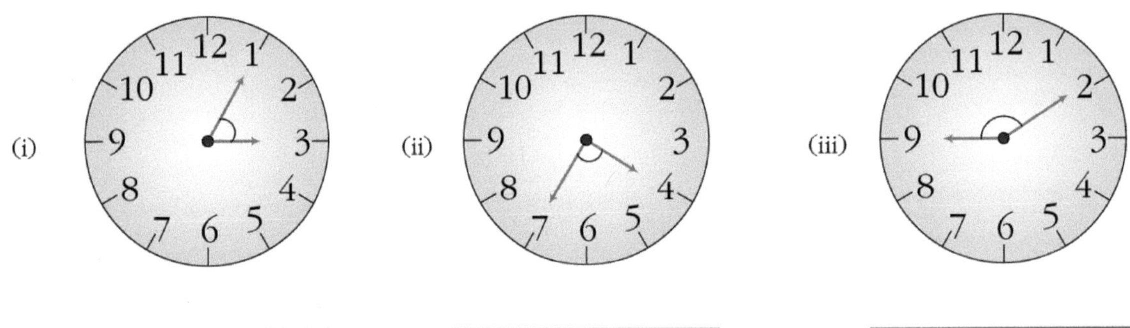

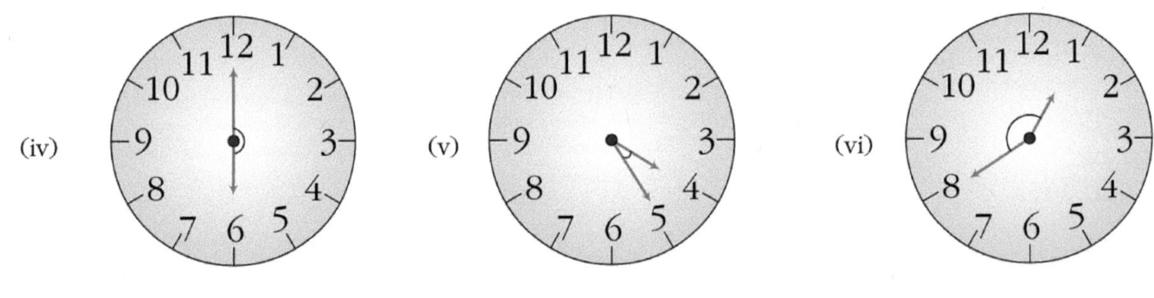

9 Draw the hands of the clock to show the following angles.

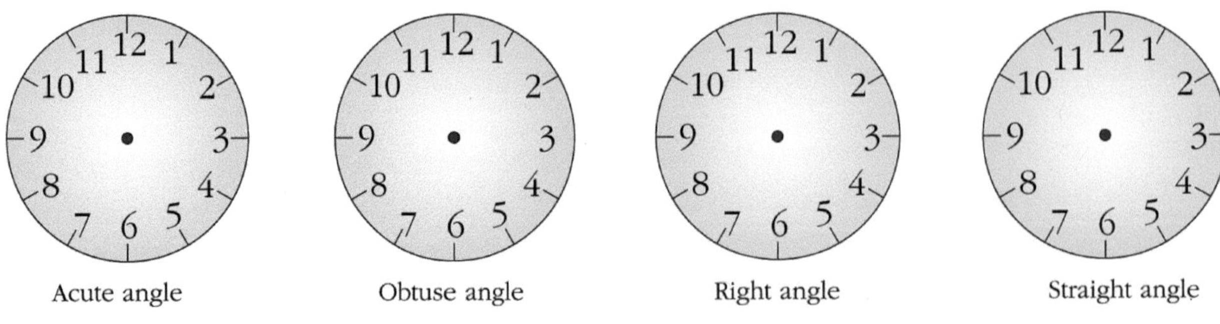

10 Measure the angle using a protractor (D).

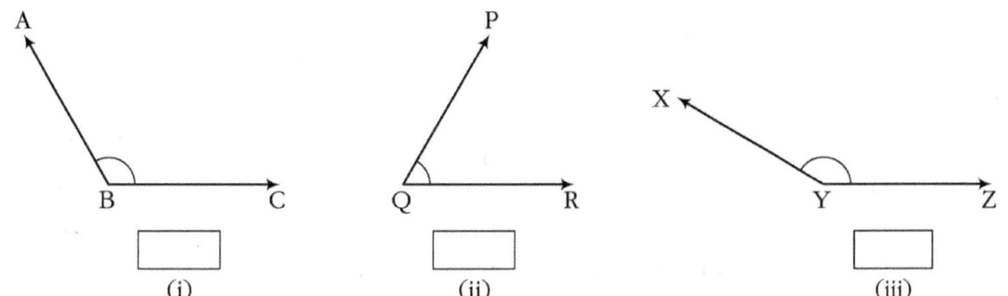

11 Draw angles whose measures are

(i) 75° (ii) 45°

(iii) 180° (iv) 135°

12 Fill in the blanks.

(i) $\frac{1}{2}$ of a right angle = ________________

(ii) ________________ of a right angle = 30°

(iii) 3 times of a right angle = ________________

(iv) ________________ times of a right angle = 180°

13 Mr. Roy asked his class to identify a mystery shape from below given shapes.

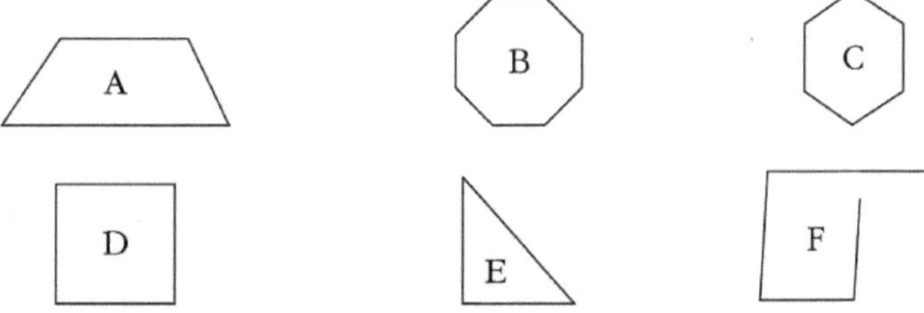

He gave the class following two clues :

I. The mystery shape is a closed figure with less than 5 sides.

II. The mystery shape does not have any 90° angle.

Which of the above shapes is the mystery shape?

____

____

14 The figure shown below is a geometrical shape. Some students make different observations about the shape as given below.

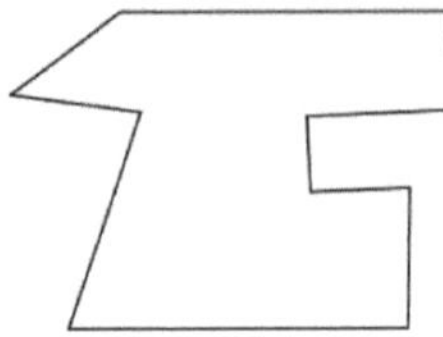

Rani : I can see 5 pairs of **perpendicular** lines.

Monu : There are 7 angles in the figure.

Sonia : There is only one pair of **parallel** lines.

Raju : 6 of the angles are less than a right angle.

Who is making the correct observation?

____

____

15 Write the letters of the English alphabet series which consists of only right angles.

16 A child was playing with matchsticks to design various shapes. He designed a shape given below.

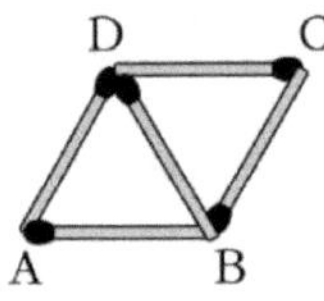

Draw a shape with the help of 8 matchsticks and write the measure of the angles formed.

[Chapter **3**]

How Many Squares?

1 Find out the perimeter of the shapes given below. One has been done for you

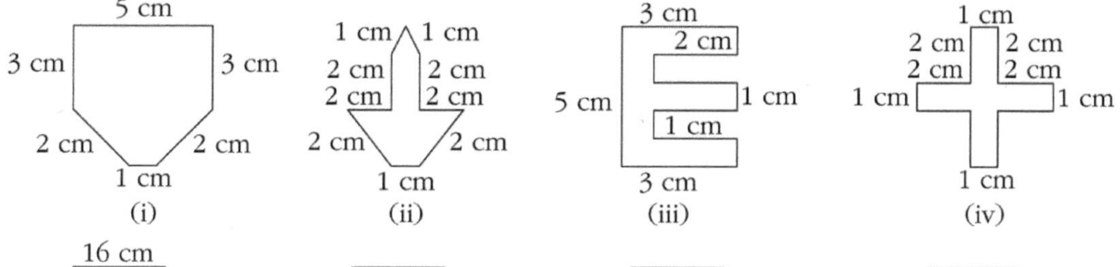

(a) Which figure has greatest (maximum) perimeter? ______

(b) Which figure has least (minimum) perimeter? ______

(c) What is the difference between the perimeter of figures (i) and (iv)? ______

2 A school boy has collected different types of postal stamps and pasted it on clip board.

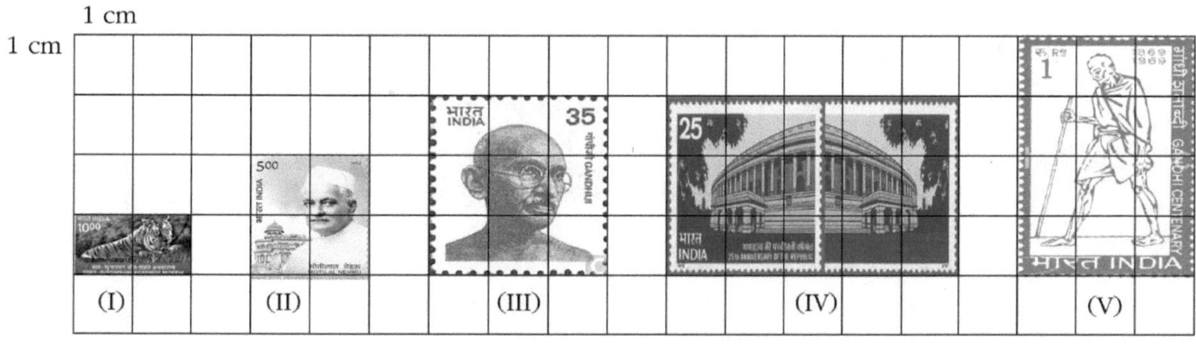

(i) Can you tell without measuring which stamp has the biggest area? Also, find its perimeter.

______

(ii) Can you tell without measuring which stamp covers least number of squares? Also, find the area of that stamp.

______

(iii) Find the difference between the area of the smallest and the biggest stamps.

______

3 Look at the outline of some leaves on the square grid given below. Find their areas and fill in the blanks that follow.

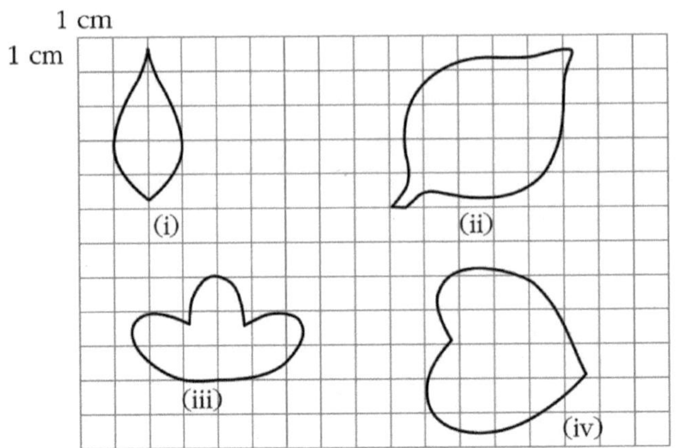

(a) The biggest leaf is _______ leaf and its area is _______ sq cm.

(b) The smallest leaf is made up of _______ squares.

4 Find the area of the following figures.

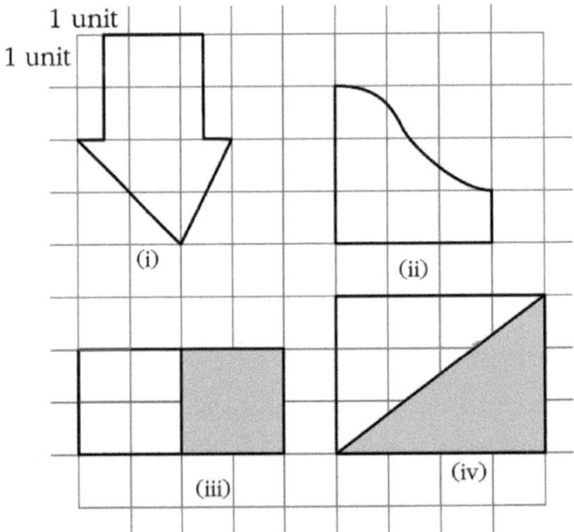

5 Count the squares enclosed and also find the perimeter of each shape.

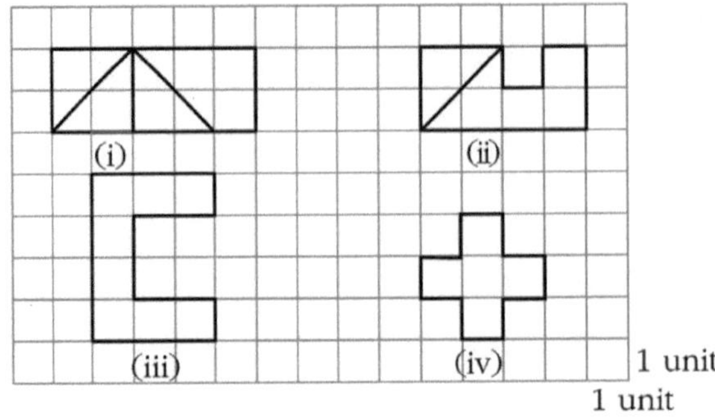

(a) Which shape has the greatest perimeter? _______________

6 Raju has drawn four shapes. Complete each shape with two more sides, so that the area of each shape is as given below it.

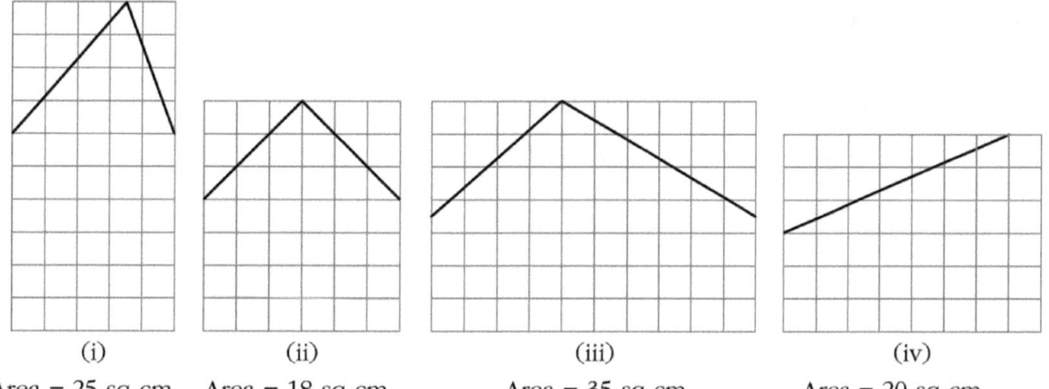

(i) Area = 25 sq cm (ii) Area = 18 sq cm (iii) Area = 35 sq cm (iv) Area = 20 sq cm

7 Draw a shape to represent the following areas. One has been done for you.

Area = 14 sq cm

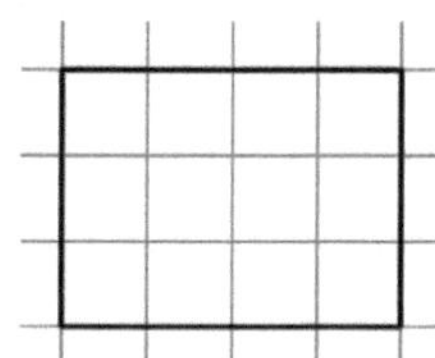

(i) Area = 18 sq cm (ii) Area = 8 sq cm

(iii) Area = 15 sq cm (iv) Area = 6 sq cm

(v) Area = 20 sq cm

8 Draw different patterns using five squares. One has been done for you.

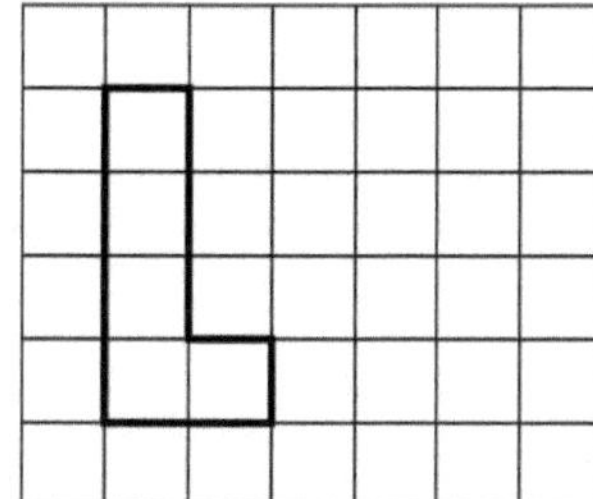

9 Apeksha wants to make some patterns using the tiles given below. Draw different patterns using the given tiles.

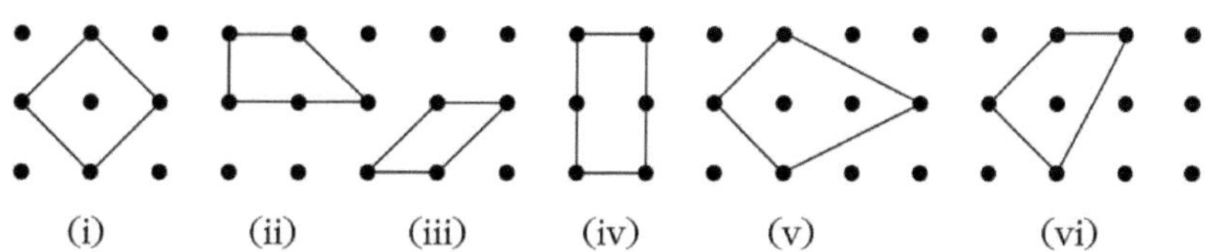

(i) (ii) (iii) (iv) (v) (vi)

10 The following is the pattern of a window of a house. Draw the tile which is being used in making the pattern.

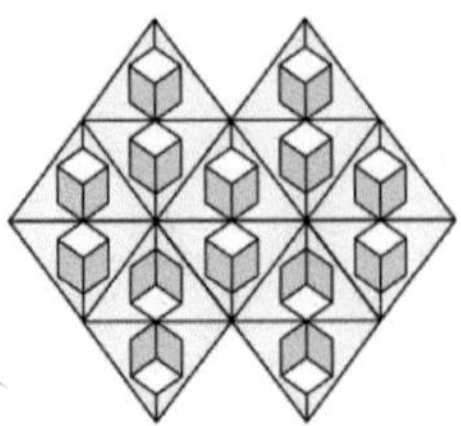

11 Make tile patterns with the help of following tiles.

12 Given below are some tiles.

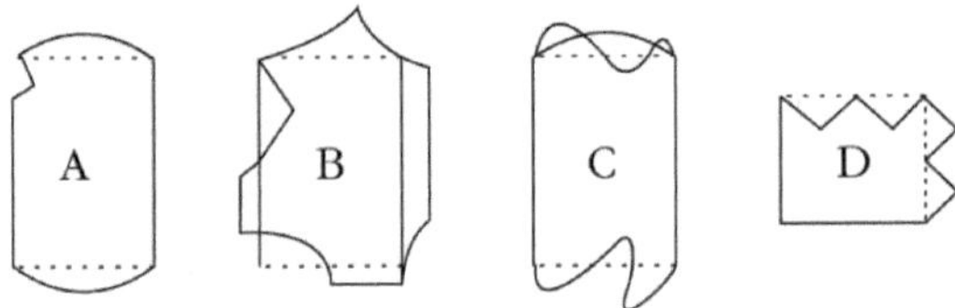

Answer the following questions on the basis of above tiles.

(i) Which of the above shapes will tile a floor without leaving any gaps?

(ii) Make design using those tiles below.

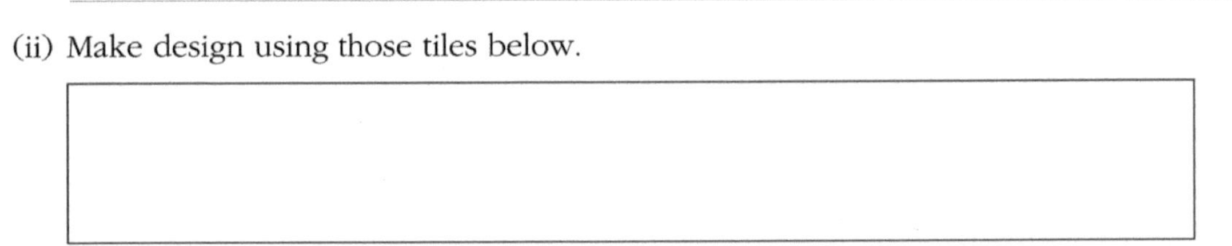

13 A farmer has a field in the shape of a rectangle as shown below. He wants to sow two types of crops in the same field. So, he divided the area into two parts (not equal) to sow wheat and oil seeds.

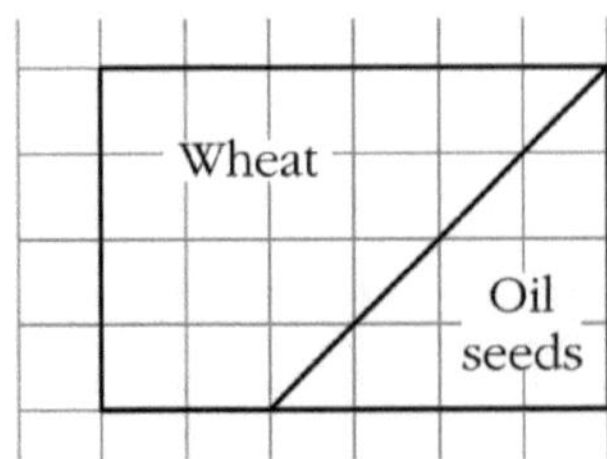

Find the area occupied by each crop. Which is bigger and by how much?

[Chapter 4]

Parts and Wholes

1 Multiple choice questions.

(i) Which of the following figures are shaded more than $\frac{1}{2}$?

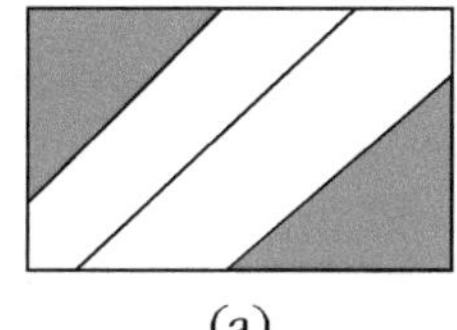
(a)

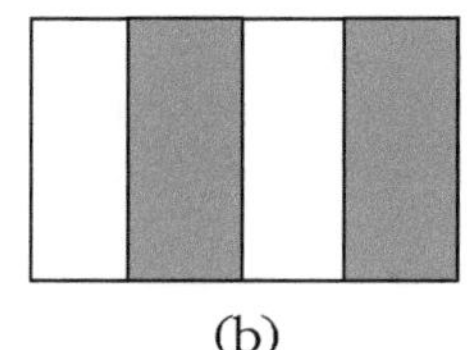
(b)

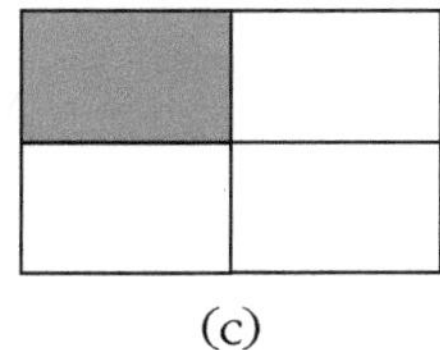
(c)

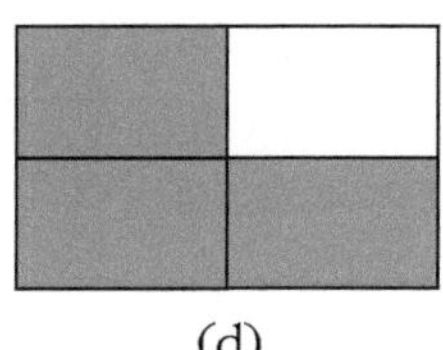
(d)

(ii) Tick the correct fraction (shaded part) shown in the below figure.

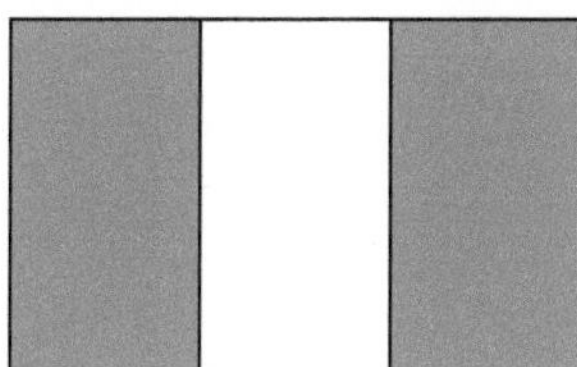

(a) $\frac{1}{3}$ (b) $\frac{2}{3}$

(c) $\frac{1}{2}$ (d) 1

(iii) Choose the correct statement to show the fraction of unshaded part.

(a) More than $\frac{3}{4}$ (b) More than $\frac{6}{7}$

(c) More than $\frac{1}{2}$ (d) Less than $\frac{1}{2}$

(iv) Choose the option representing the correct fraction of the shaded part.

(a) 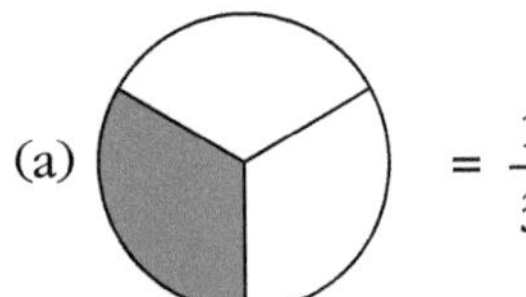 $= \frac{1}{3}$

(b) $= \frac{1}{2}$

(c) 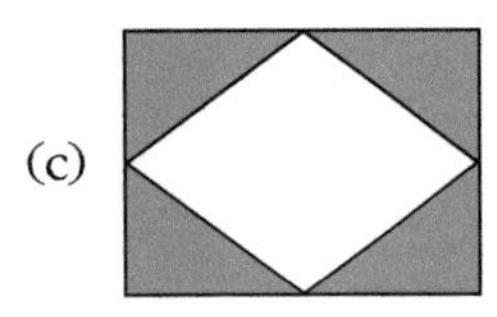 $= \frac{4}{5}$

(d) $= \frac{1}{3}$

2 **Write the fractions of the given figures. One has been done for you.**

(i) 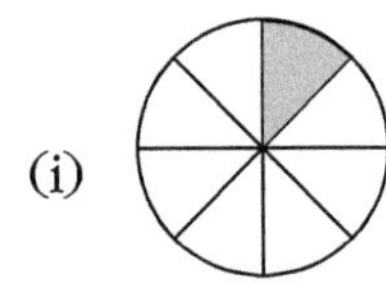

Shaded = 1/8

Unshaded = 7/8

(ii) 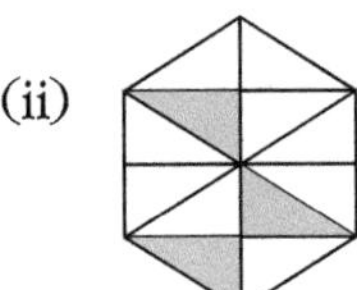

Shaded = ________

Unshaded = ________

(iii)

Shaded = ________

Unshaded = ________

(iv) 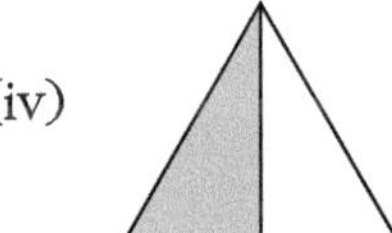

Shaded = ________

Unshaded = ________

(v) 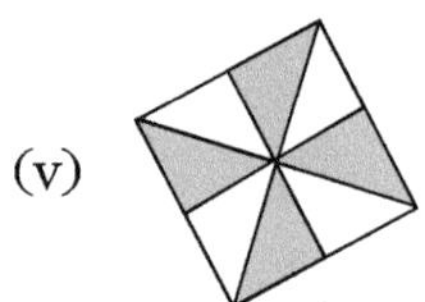

Shaded = ________

Unshaded = ________

3 **Shade the figures according to the given fractions. One has been done for you.**

(i) 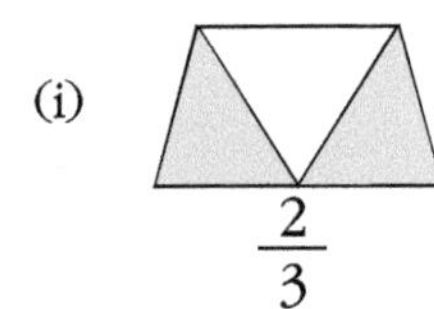

$\frac{2}{3}$

(ii)

$\frac{2}{4}$

(iii) 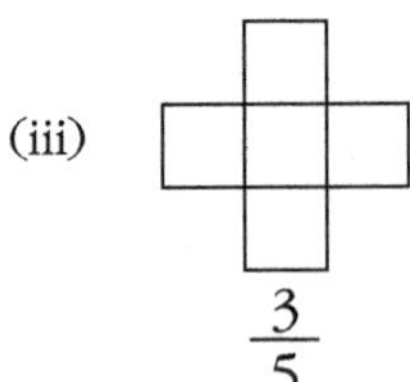

$\frac{3}{5}$

(iv) 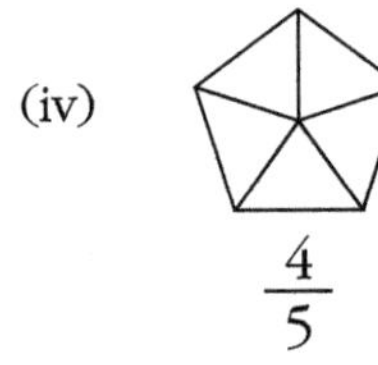

$\frac{4}{5}$

(v)

$\frac{1}{4}$

(vi) 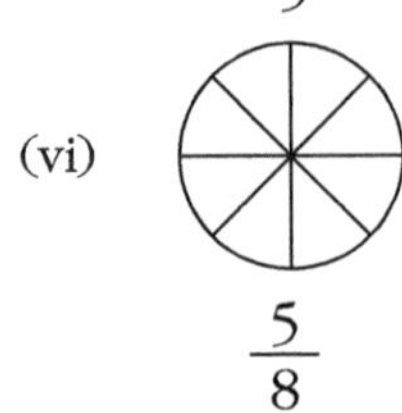

$\frac{5}{8}$

4 Look at the following grid.

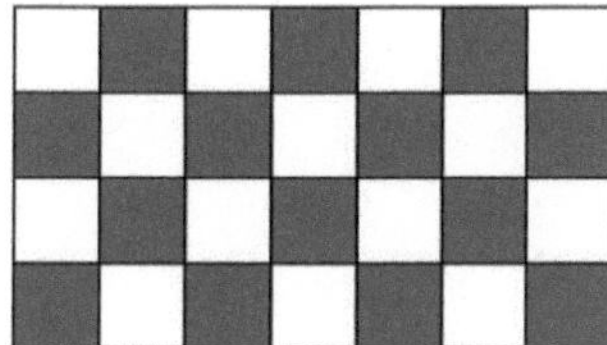

Now based on the above grid, answer the question given below.

Choose the black coloured and white coloured fraction of the grid.

(a) $\frac{1}{2}$ black, $\frac{1}{2}$ white (b) $\frac{3}{4}$ black, $\frac{1}{2}$ white

(c) $\frac{1}{2}$ black, $\frac{3}{2}$ white (d) $\frac{3}{2}$ black, $\frac{4}{2}$ white

5 **Maria divided her garden area into 9 equal parts and grew different flowers on it as shown below.**

Sunflower	Rose	Lily
Bluebell	Sunflower	Marigold
Lily	Rose	Sunflower

Answer the following questions on the basis of above information.

(i) Which flower occupies the biggest part of her garden? How much part is occupied?

(ii) On what part of the garden does she grow rose flowers?

(iii) What part of the garden does she grow bluebell?

(iv) Which two flowers cover an area of $\frac{2}{9}$ each?

6 Garima had 15 bananas and 20 apples. She distributed these fruits among Raju, Mohan and Sonia. She gave $\frac{1}{5}$ of the bananas and $\frac{3}{10}$ of the apples to Raju. Mohan got $\frac{2}{5}$ of the bananas and $\frac{1}{10}$ of the apples. Remaining fruits were given to Sonia. Find

(i) how many apples did Raju get?

(ii) how many bananas did Mohan get?

(iii) what is the share of apples and bananas which Sonia got?

7 Laxman had ₹ 1200 in his pocket. He spent half of money on breakfast, then $\frac{1}{3}$rd of remaining on buying a jeans and after that $\frac{1}{4}$th of remaining on goggles. How much money is he left with?

8 Classify the fractions given below, which are equivalent to $\frac{1}{2}, \frac{2}{3}, \frac{3}{4}, \frac{2}{5}$ and $\frac{1}{3}$, separately.

$\frac{20}{40}$, $\frac{13}{26}$, $\frac{16}{24}$, $\frac{12}{24}$, $\frac{14}{35}$, $\frac{30}{45}$,

$\frac{24}{36}$, $\frac{4}{10}$, $\frac{36}{48}$, $\frac{27}{36}$, $\frac{9}{12}$, $\frac{15}{20}$,

$\frac{22}{55}$, $\frac{6}{15}$, $\frac{10}{25}$, $\frac{20}{50}$, $\frac{18}{45}$, $\frac{8}{24}$, $\frac{16}{40}$

9 Check whether the fractions given in each part are equivalent or not.

(i) $\frac{7}{14}$ and $\frac{5}{10}$ (ii) $\frac{5}{55}$ and $\frac{11}{121}$ (iii) $\frac{8}{13}$ and $\frac{6}{11}$ (iv) $\frac{10}{14}$ and $\frac{25}{35}$

10 Application based questions.

(i) A coat costs ₹ 400. A shopkeeper gives a discount of $\frac{3}{10}$ on the price. How much will Raju pay to buy the coat?

(ii) A family buys $3\frac{2}{5}$ m and $2\frac{1}{5}$ m of cloth for two dresses. If each of them costs ₹ 15 per m, then what will be the total cost?

(iii) Sonu and Samuel took 45 min to reach school. If they walked for $\frac{1}{3}$ of the time and went by bus for the remaining time, how many minutes did they spend in the bus?

(iv) A rope has a length of 35 m. A person wants to cut the rope into some pieces of $3\frac{1}{2}$ m each. Find the number of pieces of rope that can be cut.

(v) Seema uses $\frac{1}{4}$ kg paneer to serve 4 people. How much paneer will be needed to serve 12 people?

____

____

11 Solve the following.

(i) $\frac{1}{4}$ of ₹ 1 = __________ paise

(ii) $\frac{1}{3}$ of ₹ 150 = ₹ __________

(iii) $\frac{2}{5}$ of ₹ 2 = __________ paise

(iv) $\frac{4}{5}$ of ₹ 100 = ₹ __________

(v) 50 seconds = __________ of a minute

(vi) 75 paise = __________ of ₹ 1

(vii) 4 hours = __________ of a day

(viii) 1 day = __________ of a week

(ix) $\frac{1}{7}$ of 2100 g = __________ of 1 kg

12 Kirti wants to buy vegetables according to the list given by her mother. She looks at the price list board.

Price List

Item	**Price** (in ₹ per kg)
Potato	8
Onion	18
Tomato	16
Carrot	10
Cauliflower	12
Brinjal	20

Answer the following questions on the basis of above price list.

(i) How much does 3 kg of tomato cost? ______

(ii) How must does $\frac{1}{4}$ kg of tomato cost? ______

(iii) If she wants to buy $2\frac{1}{2}$ kg of potato. How much will it cost? ______

(iv) How much does $4\frac{1}{2}$ kg of carrot cost? ______

(v) If she wants to buy

(a) 2 kg of tomato.

(b) $3\frac{1}{2}$ kg of onion.

(c) $1\frac{1}{4}$ kg of brinjal.

(d) 1 kg of carrot.

(e) $\frac{1}{2}$ kg of cauliflower.

(f) $4\frac{3}{4}$ kg of potato.

Now, prepare a bill for her.

Item	**Price** (in ₹ per kg)	**Amount** (in ₹)
Total		

13 State 'True' or 'False'.

	True/False		True/False
(i) $\frac{3}{4}$ of a dozen is 10.	______	(ii) $\frac{1}{2}$ of a decade is 5.	______
(iii) $\frac{1}{3}$ of a year is 4 months.	______	(iv) $\frac{3}{5}$ of a rupee is 60 paise.	______
(v) $\frac{1}{2}$ of a day is 4 hours.	______	(vi) $\frac{2}{3}$ of an hour is 40 min.	______
(vii) $\frac{2}{5}$ of a kilogram is 500 g.	______	(viii) $\frac{1}{4}$ of a litre is 250 mL.	______

[Chapter **5**]

Does It Look the Same?

1 Draw the line(s) to divide the shapes given below into mirror halves. Also, find how many such lines can be drawn. One has been done for your.

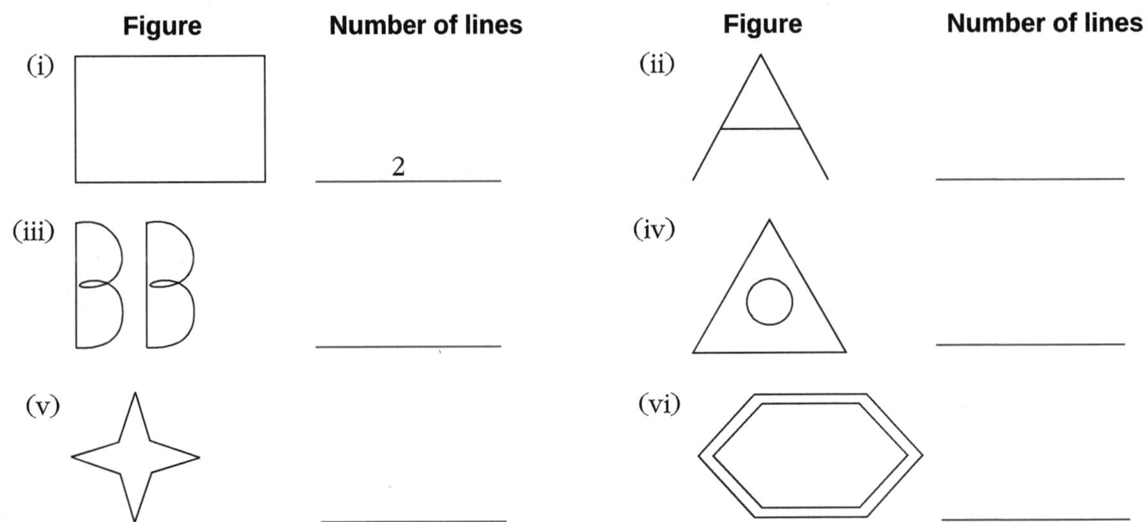

2 Draw the mirror image of the following. (Mirror is placed along the dotted line)

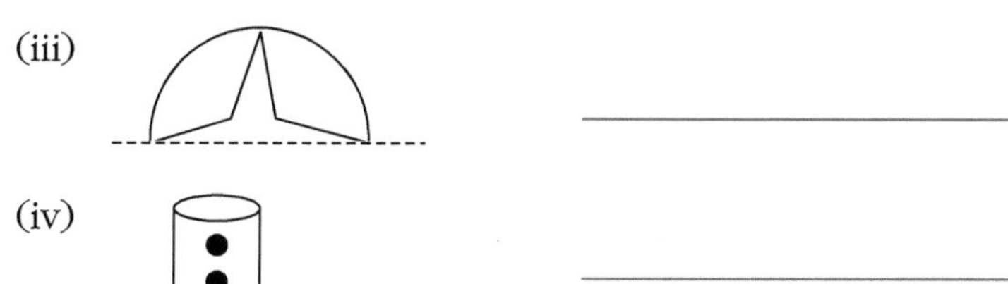

3 State, whether the following figures can be divided into mirror halves or not.

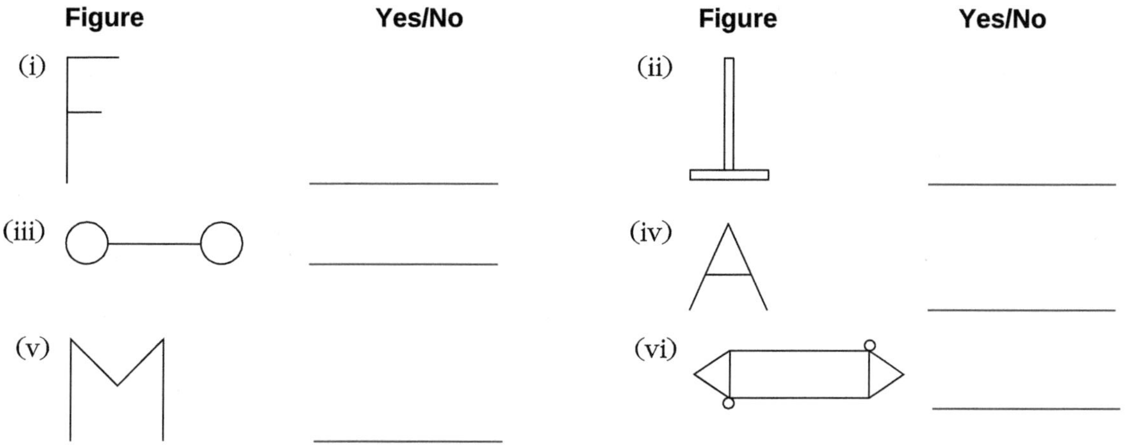

4 State, whether the following figures has been correctly divided into mirror halves or not. One has been done for you.

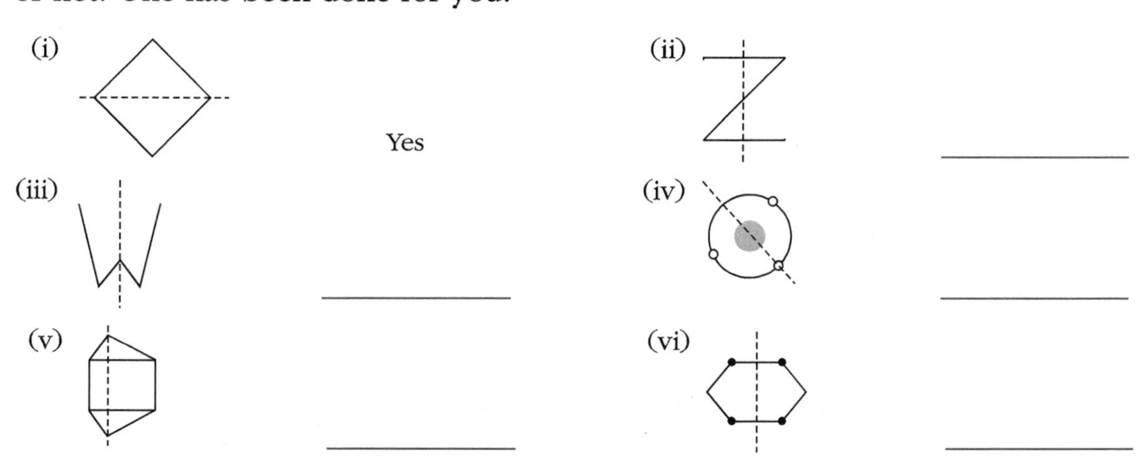

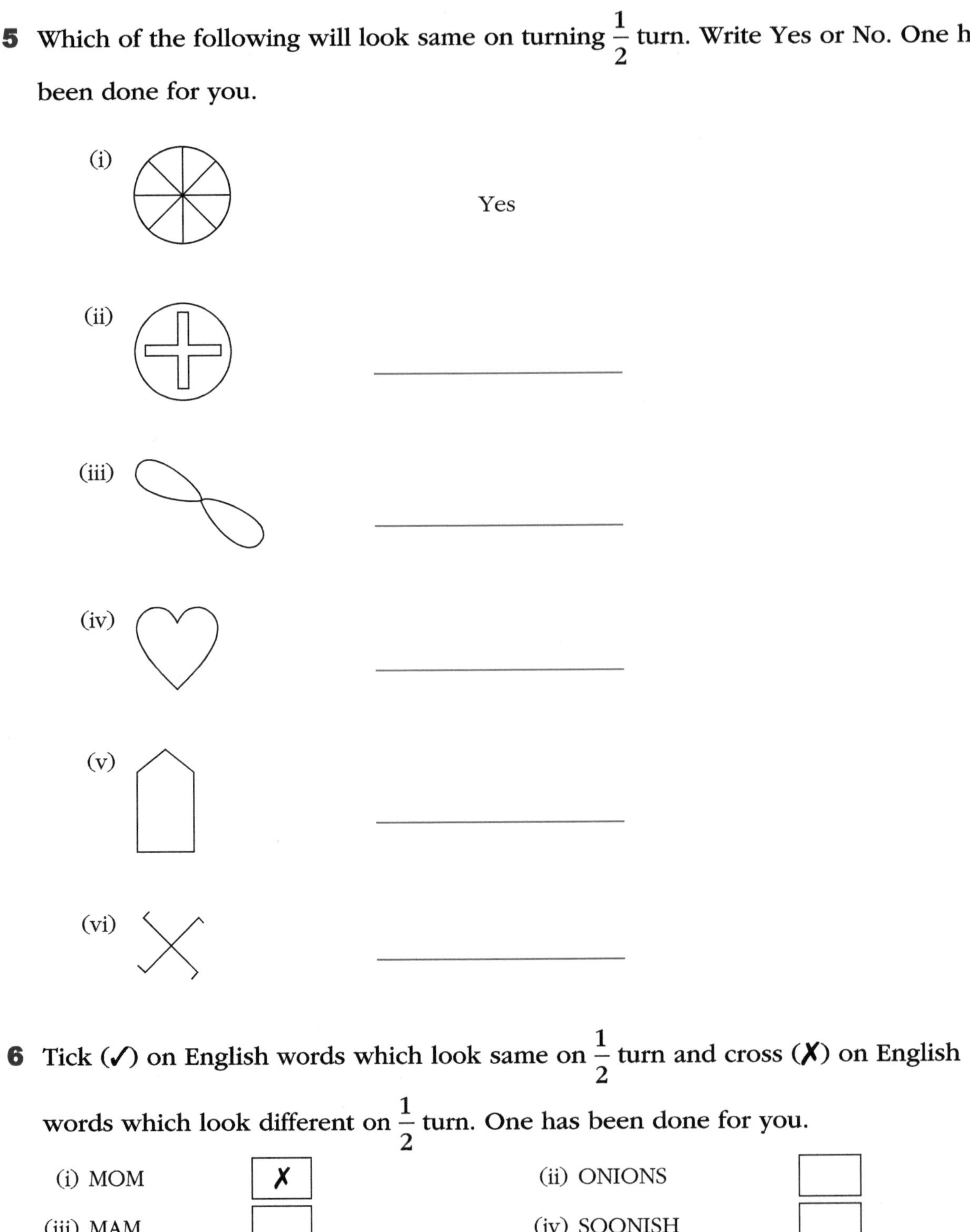

5 Which of the following will look same on turning $\frac{1}{2}$ turn. Write Yes or No. One has been done for you.

(i) Yes

(ii) ______________

(iii) ______________

(iv) ______________

(v) ______________

(vi) ______________

6 Tick (✓) on English words which look same on $\frac{1}{2}$ turn and cross (✗) on English words which look different on $\frac{1}{2}$ turn. One has been done for you.

(i) MOM	✗	(ii) ONIONS	
(iii) MAM		(iv) SOONISH	
(v) SWIMS		(vi) SIS	

7 Some numbers are given below. Which of the following will look same after making $\frac{1}{2}$ turn? Tick (✓) them.

(i) 111 ____________ (ii) 101 ____________

(iii) 3333 ____________ (iv) 1111 ____________

(v) 10001 ____________ (vi) 999 ____________

8 Look at the figures and draw its shape after following the instructions given below.

(i) 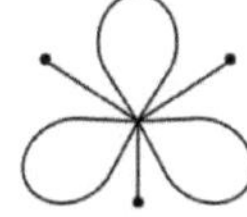 $\frac{1}{2}$ turn ____________ $\frac{1}{4}$ turn ____________

(ii) 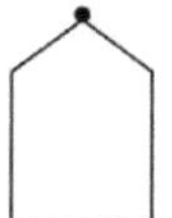 $\frac{1}{2}$ turn ____________ $\frac{1}{4}$ turn ____________

(iii) 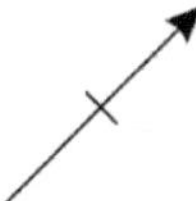 $\frac{1}{2}$ turn ____________ $\frac{1}{4}$ turn ____________

9 Tick (✓) the figures which will look same on the turning and cross (✗) which will look different on the turning.

(i)  $\frac{1}{3}$ turn = ☐

(ii)  $\frac{1}{6}$ turn = ☐

(iii) 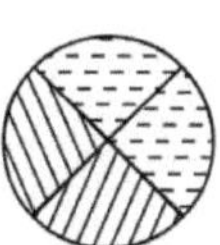 $\frac{1}{2}$ turn = ☐

(iv) 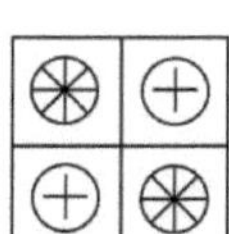 $\frac{1}{4}$ turn = ☐

(v) 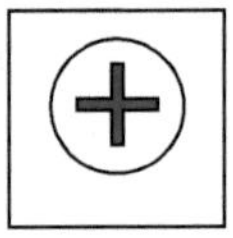 $\frac{1}{4}$ turn =

(vi)  $\frac{1}{6}$ turn =

(vii) 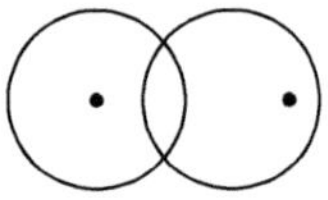 $\frac{1}{2}$ turn =

(viii)  $\frac{1}{6}$ turn =

(ix) 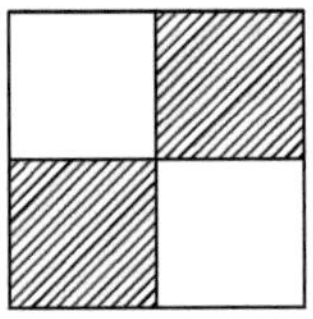 $\frac{1}{4}$ turn =

(x)  $\frac{1}{2}$ turn =

(xi)  $\frac{1}{3}$ turn =

(xii) 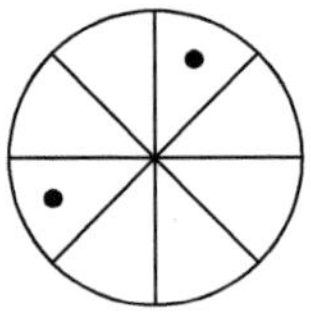 $\frac{1}{2}$ turn =

(xiii) 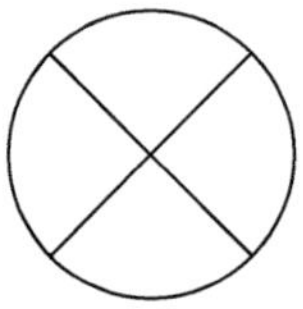 $\frac{1}{2}$ turn =

(xiv) 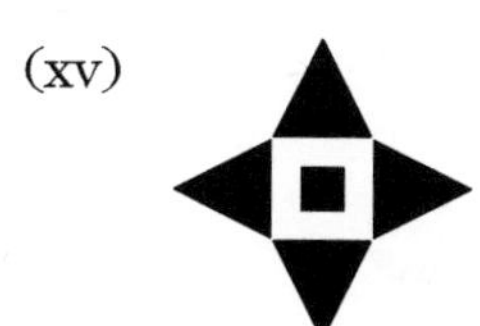 $\frac{1}{3}$ turn =

(xv) $\frac{1}{4}$ turn =

(xvi) $\frac{1}{2}$ turn =

(xvii) $\frac{1}{6}$ turn =

(xviii) $\frac{1}{6}$ turn =

[Chapter **6**]

Be My Multiple, I'll be Your Factor

1 Samantha is trying to catch Krimmy. Krimmy is on the 16th step and can jump 2 steps at a time. Samantha is on the 6th step and can jump 3 steps at a time. If Krimmy reaches the 30th step, then she wins.

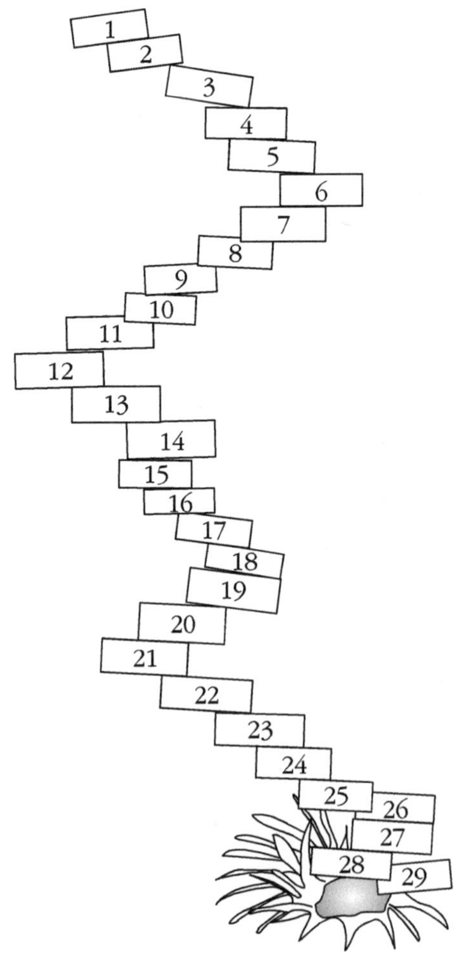

Answer the following questions on the basis of given diagram.

(i) The steps on which Krimmy jumps ______________

(ii) The steps on which Samantha jumps ______________

(iii) The steps on which both Samantha and Krimmy jumps are ______________

(iv) Does Krimmy win? ______________

2 **Rohan's mother asked him to find the answer of riddle by using the given table of number. See asked him to make a cross above the numbers which are multiple of 5, a tick above the numbers which are multiple of 4 and a dot above the numbers which are multiple of 2.**

1	2	3	4	5	6	7	8	9	10
11	12	13	14	(C) 15	16 (B)	17	18	19	(F) 20
21	(R) 22	23	24	25	26	27	(M) 28	29	30
31	32	33	34	35	36	37	38	39	(A) 40
(O) 41	42	43	(B) 44	45	(C) 46	47	48	49	50
51	52	53	54	55	56	57	58	59	(C) 60
61	62	63	64	65	(A) 66	67	68	69	70
71	72	(C) 73	74	75	76	77	(O) 78	79	(T) 80
81	82	83	84	85	86	87	88	89	90
91	92	(T) 93	94	95	96	(T) 97	98	99	(O) 100
101	102	103	104	(F) 105	106	107	108	(N) 109	110
111	112	113	(B) 114	115	116	(T) 117	118	119	(R) 120

Now, write the letters which have all the three marks – a cross, a tick and a dot. What is the word formed from those letters?

3 **Write the next 5 multiples of each of the following given numbers.**

	1st	2nd	3rd	4th	5th
(i) 3	______	______	______	______	______
(ii) 5	______	______	______	______	______
(iii) 11	______	______	______	______	______
(iv) 14	______	______	______	______	______
(v) 18	______	______	______	______	______

4 Some numbers are given below

2	3	4	5	6	7	8	9	10	11
12	13	14	15	16	17	18	19	20	21
22	23	24	25	26	27	28	29	30	31
32	33	34	35	36	37	38	39	40	41
42	43	44	45	46	47	48	49		

(i) Circle the numbers which are multiples of 3.

(ii) Tick the numbers which are multiples of 4.

(iii) Cross the numbers which are multiples of 6.

(iv) Write the numbers which are multiples of 3, 4 and 6.

5 Fill in the blanks by writing the first common multiples. One has been done for you.

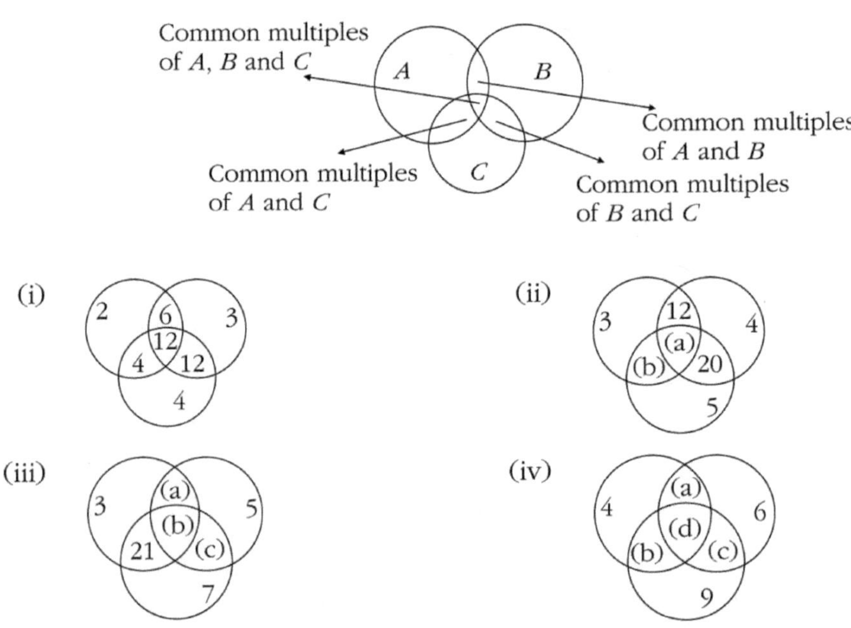

6 Write first three common multiples of the given numbers.

	1st	**2nd**	**3rd**
(i) 2, 3	________	________	________
(ii) 3, 5	________	________	________
(iii) 5, 7	________	________	________

7 Find the smallest common multiple of the following numbers.

(i) 24, 12 = ____________ (ii) 16, 12 = ____________

(iii) 50, 25, 75 = ____________ (iv) 6, 18, 12 = ____________

8 Fill in the blanks.

	Number	Factors (including the number)	Number of factors
(i)	8	____________	____________
(ii)	12	____________	____________
(iii)	15	____________	____________
(iv)	20	____________	____________
(v)	17	____________	____________
(vi)	19	____________	____________

9 Write the common factors of the given pairs of numbers.

(i) 8, 10 = ____________ (ii) 12, 18 = ____________

(iii) 20, 25 = ____________ (iv) 40, 56 = ____________

(v) 50, 60 = ____________ (vi) 45, 75 = ____________

10 Check whether the numbers given below are divisible by the given digits or not and put tick (✓) or cross (✗).

Number	2	3	4	5	6	8	10
7326	✓	✓	✗	✗			
3103	✗	✗					
642							
48400							
39635							

11 Write the common factor(s) of the given numbers in the middle and remaining factors in their circles respectively (excluding 1 and the number itself). One has been done for you.

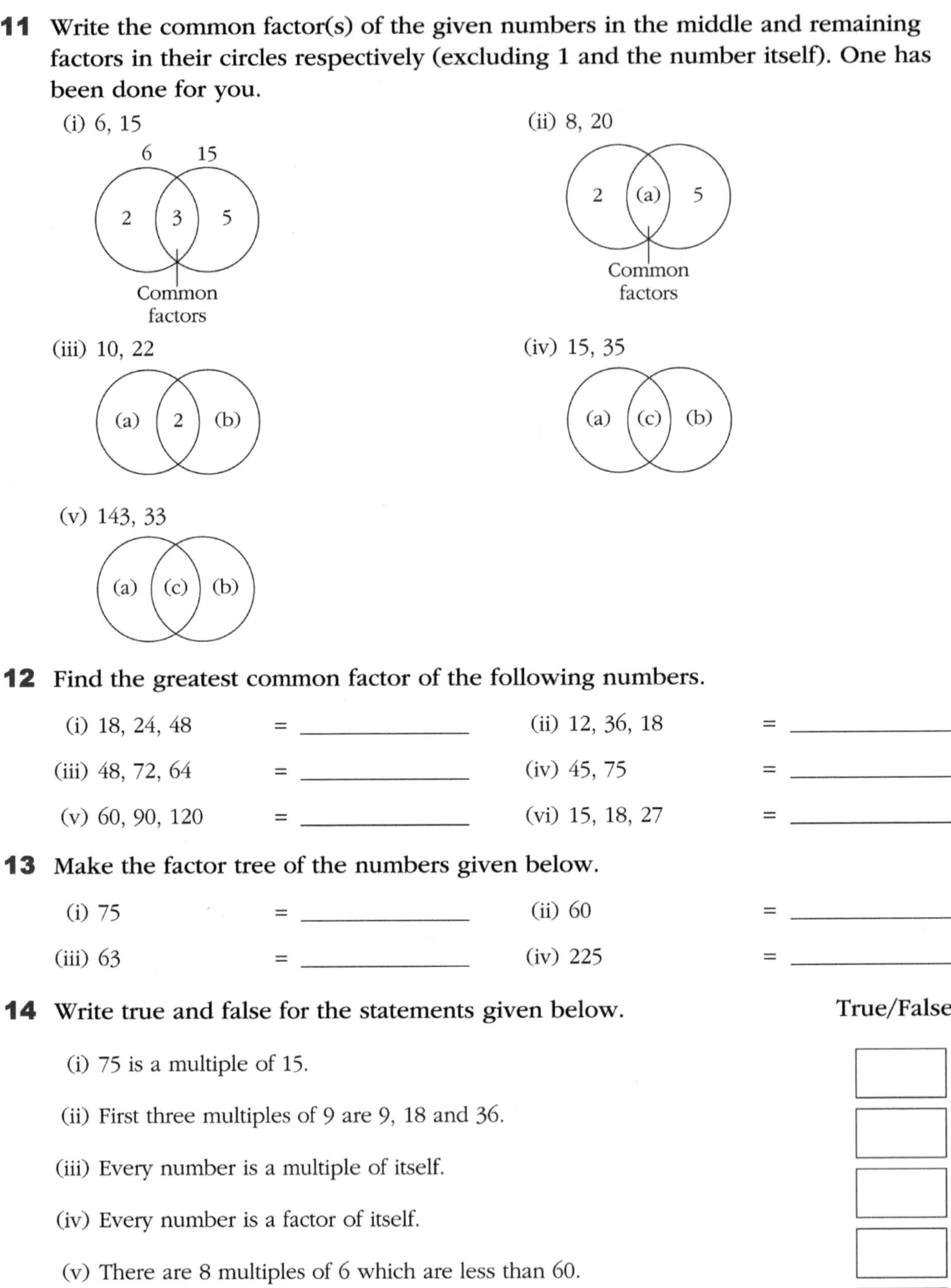

12 Find the greatest common factor of the following numbers.

(i) 18, 24, 48 = ____________ (ii) 12, 36, 18 = ____________

(iii) 48, 72, 64 = ____________ (iv) 45, 75 = ____________

(v) 60, 90, 120 = ____________ (vi) 15, 18, 27 = ____________

13 Make the factor tree of the numbers given below.

(i) 75 = ____________ (ii) 60 = ____________

(iii) 63 = ____________ (iv) 225 = ____________

14 Write true and false for the statements given below. True/False

(i) 75 is a multiple of 15. ☐

(ii) First three multiples of 9 are 9, 18 and 36. ☐

(iii) Every number is a multiple of itself. ☐

(iv) Every number is a factor of itself. ☐

(v) There are 8 multiples of 6 which are less than 60. ☐

(vi) 16, 24 and 32 are consecutive multiples of 8. ☐

15 Word problems.

(i) What is the smallest common multiple of 6, 5 and 8?

(ii) There are three buckets containing 24 L, 36 L and 48 L of milk. Find the capacity of smallest bucket that can measure the milk in the three buckets.

(iii) Megha bought some chocolates. She could arrange them in any of the boxes having space for 4 chocolates, 5 chocolates and 7 chocolates. What is the minimum number of chocolates she must have bought?

(iv) What is the least number of chocolates a teacher should have so that when he distributes equal number of them to his 10, 15 or 20 students, no chocolate is left?

(v) Raju took some chocolates. He made groups with 5 of them and found 1 chocolate was left. He also tried making groups of 6 and 8 and each time 1 chocolate was left over. What is smallest number of chocolates Raju had?

(vi) Rahul decided to tile the path from his house to garage with the tiles of length 3 ft, 4 ft and 5 ft. The Mason tiled the first row with 5 ft tiles, second row with 3 ft tiles and third row with 4 ft tiles without cutting any of the tiles. What can be the shortest length of the path?

[Chapter 7]

Can You See the Pattern?

1 What will come next? One has been done for you

(i) 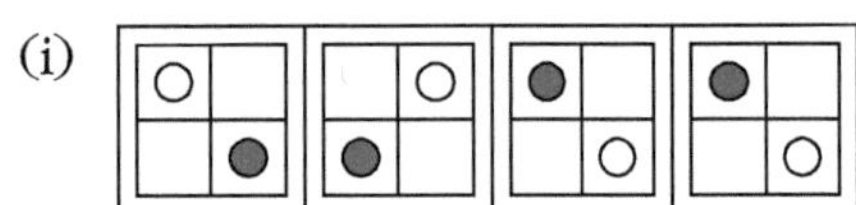

(ii) 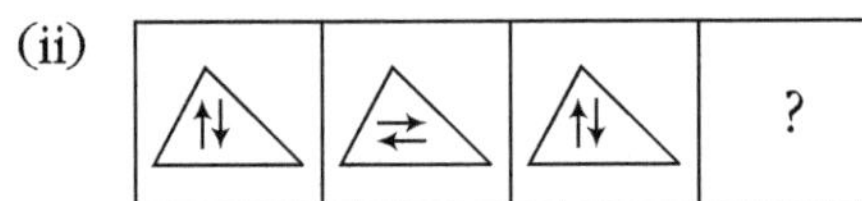

(iii) 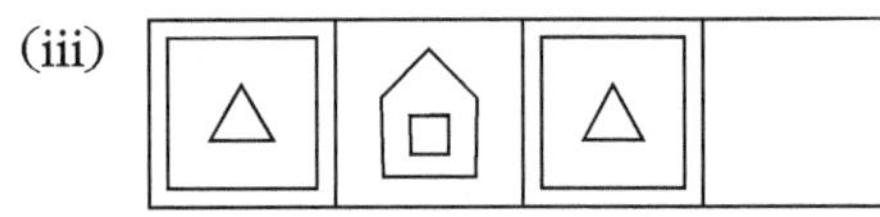

(iv) 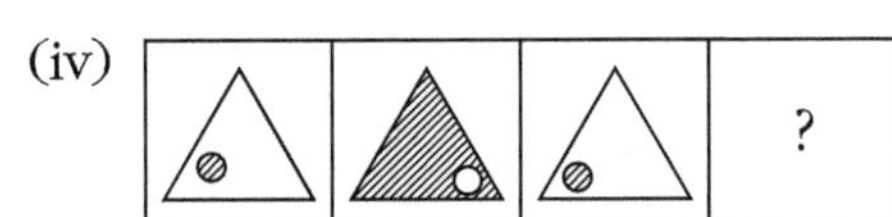

(v) 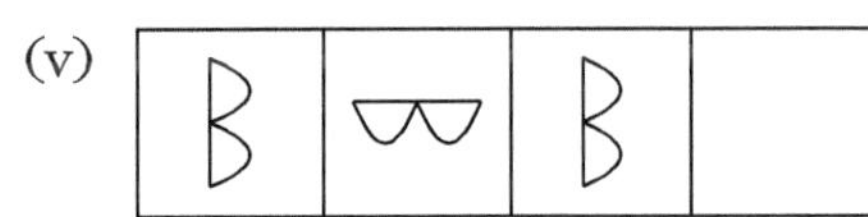

2 Complete the pattern in each part using the rule given below.

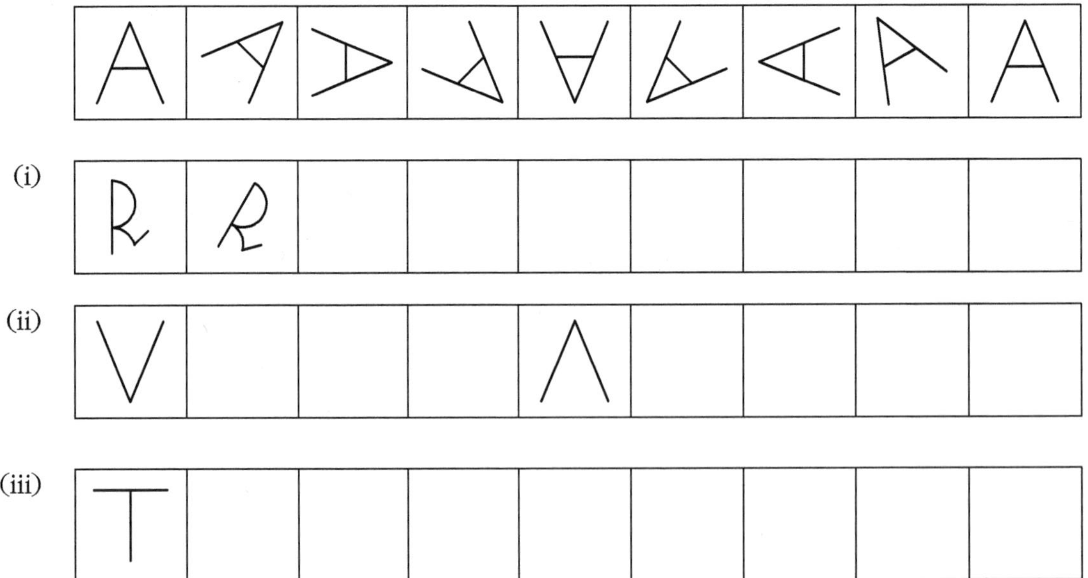

After how many steps the original figure is obtained? ____________

3 Find the rule and choose the next figure.

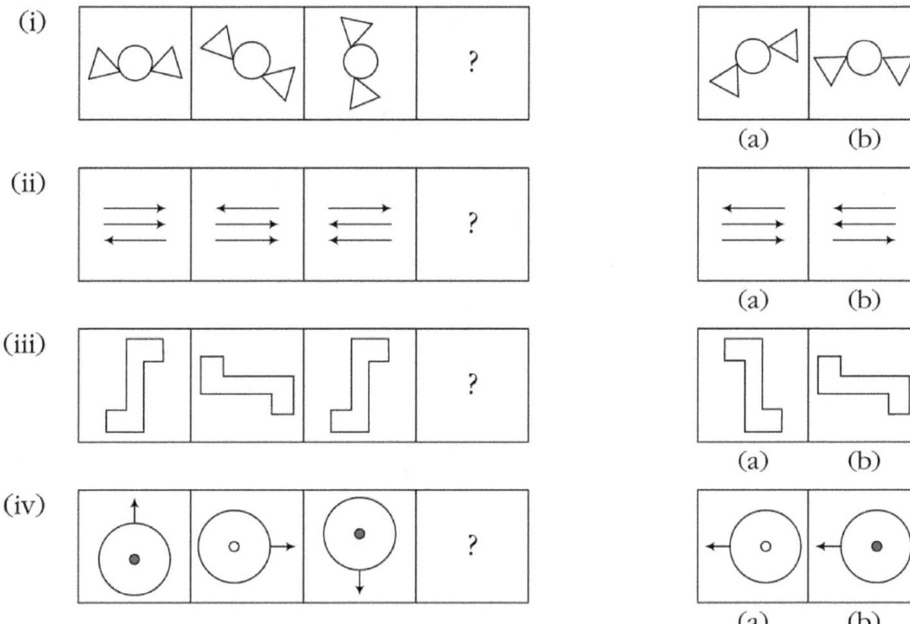

4 Observe the rule in the given patterns and tick the figure which does not follow the rule.

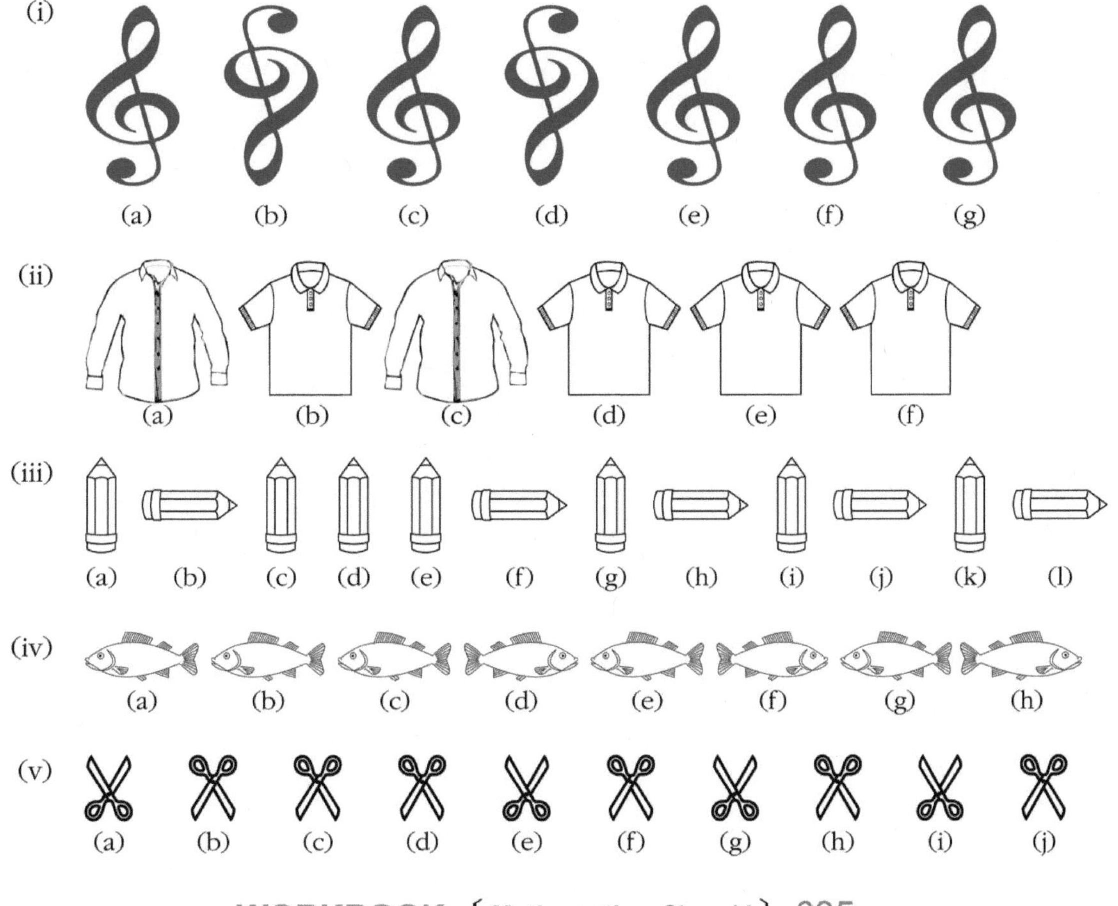

5 **Magic squares.**

Fill in the boxes below as per the instructions given.

(i)

		3
	9	
6		10

Use numbers 3 to 11.

Rule : The total of each line is 21.

(ii)

13		11
		7
	10	

Use numbers 6 to 14.

Rule : The total of each line is 30.

6 **Find the rule and complete the hexagon.**

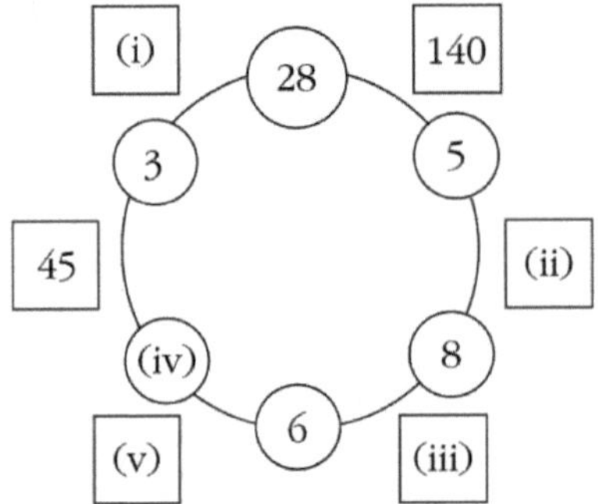

7 **Fill in the missing numbers.**

(i)

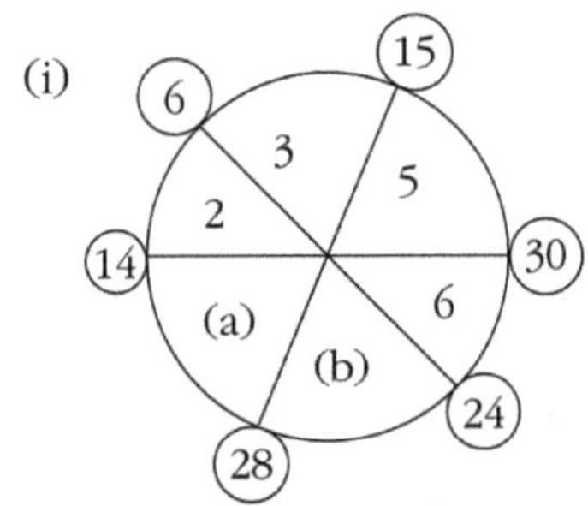

(ii)

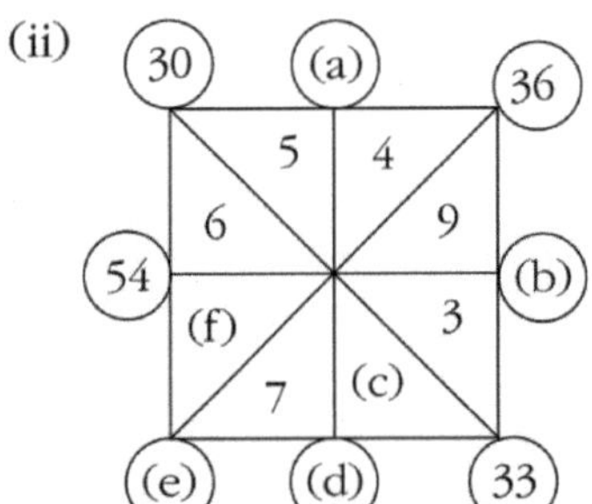

8 **Study the pattern and fill in the blanks. One has been done for you.**

(i) 24 + 37 + 19 = 37 + 24 + 19

(ii) 34 + ___ + 10 = 26 + 10 + ___

(iii) 400 + ___ + ___ = 300 + ___ + 600

(iv) 600 + ___ + 120 = ___ + ___ + 145

9 **Make special numbers.**

Change the following numbers into special numbers using the instructions given. One has been done for you.

(i) 54 — Take number 54
Turn it back to front 45
Now, add both the numbers to get 99.

(ii) 62

(iii) 234

(iv) 543

10 **See the pattern and fill in the blanks.**

(i) $27 \times 3 = 81$

$27 \times 6 = 162$

$27 \times 9 = 243$

$27 \times 12 =$ ________

$27 \times 18 =$ ________

$27 \times 24 =$ ________

(ii) $1 \times 8 + 1 = 9$

$11 \times 8 + 1 = 89$

$111 \times 8 + 1 = 889$

$1111 \times 8 + 1 =$ ________

$11111 \times 8 + 1 =$ ________

11 **Fill in the blanks.**

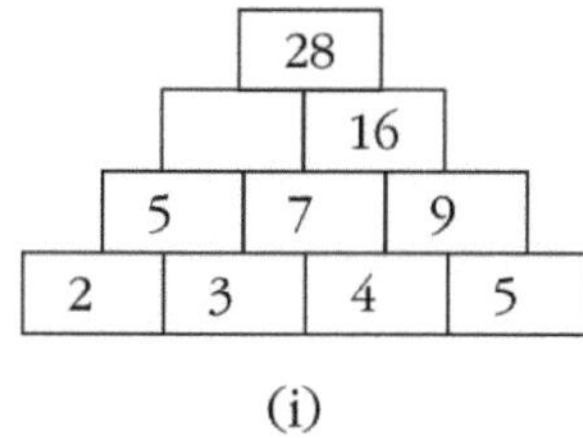

(i)

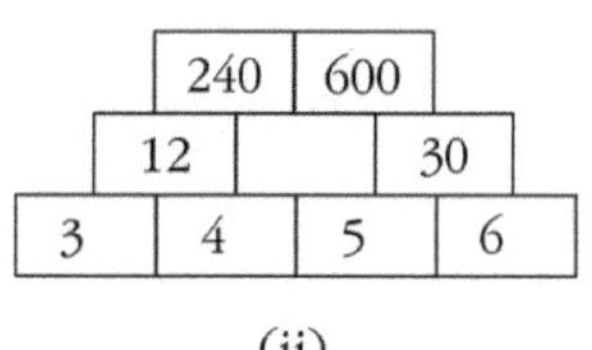

(ii)

12 **Follow the pattern given below and fill in the boxes.**

$(3 \times 3) - (2 \times 2) =$ 5

$(5 \times 5) - (4 \times 4) =$ 9

$(6 \times 6) - (5 \times 5) =$ 11

(i) $(8 \times 8) - (7 \times 7) = \square$

(ii) $(13 \times 13) - (12 \times 12) = \square$

(iii) $(15 \times 15) - (14 \times 14) = \square$

(iv) $(25 \times 25) - (24 \times 24) = \square$

13 Complete the following blanks by observing the pattern.

(i) $1 \times 1 = 1$

$11 \times 11 = 121$

(a) $111 \times 111 = \square$

(b) $\square \times \square = 1234321$

(ii) $1 \times 8 = 9 - 1$

$12 \times 8 = 98 - 2$

$123 \times 8 = 987 - 3$

(a) $\square \times 8 = 9876 - \square$

(b) $12345 \times 8 = \square - \square$

(iii) $1 + 3 = 2 \times 2$

$1 + 3 + 5 = 3 \times 3$

$1 + 3 + 5 + 7 = 4 \times 4$

(a) $\square = 7 \times 7$

(b) $1 + 3 + 5 + 7 + 9 + 11 + 13 + 15 + 17 + 19 =$

[Chapter 8]

Mapping Your Way

1 Study the following map and answer the questions that follow.

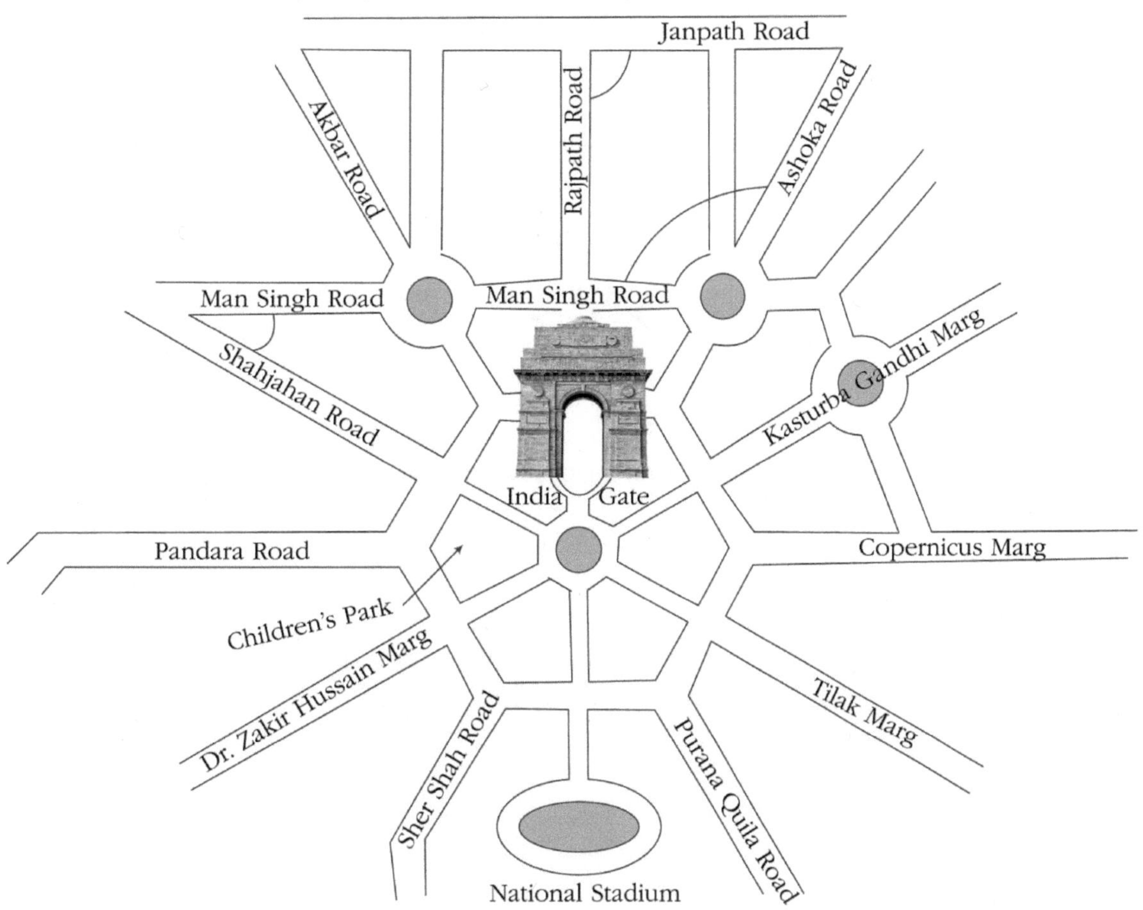

(i) What is the measure of the angle formed between Rajpath and Janpath roads?

(ii) What is the angle formed between Man Singh road and Shahjahan road?

(iii) Which geometrical shape is formed by Janpath, Akbar, Man Singh and Ashoka roads?

2 Study the following map and answer the given questions. [1 cm = 1 km]

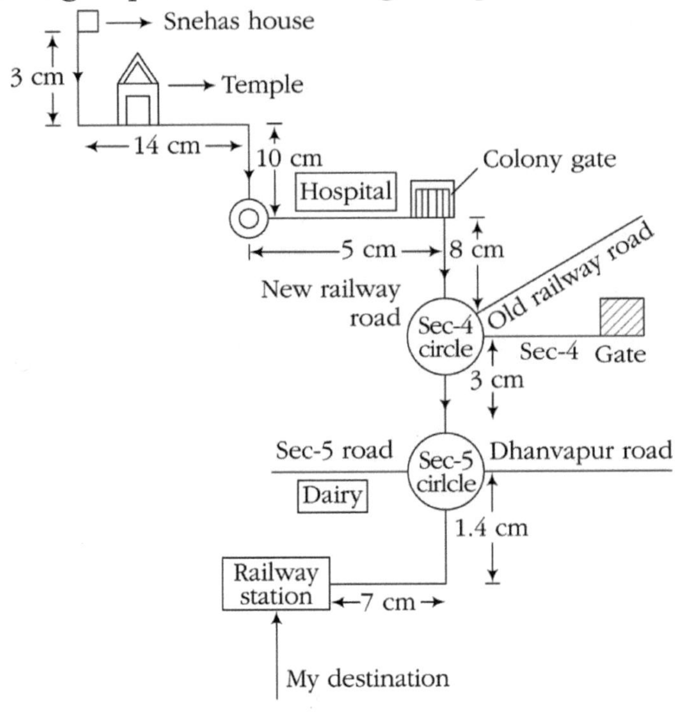

(i) Find the distance (in km) between Sneha's house and the colony gate.

(ii) If you go from sec-5 to Dhanvapur road, then in which direction will you go?

3 Arihant is situated in front of DM office in Daryaganj. DM office is to the left side of Red Fort as shown in the map given below [1 cm = 15 km]

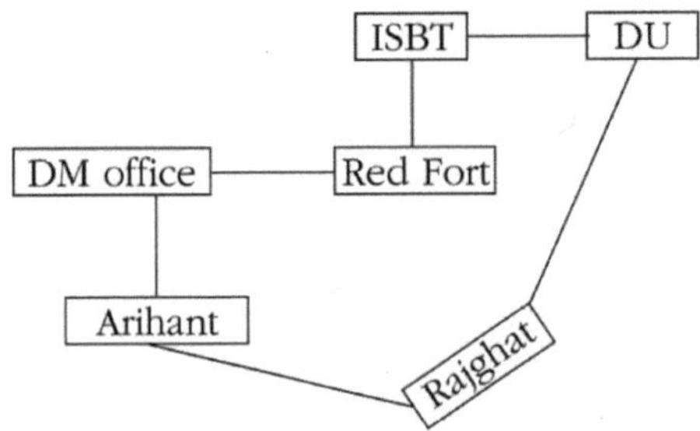

(i) Rohit lives in Daryaganj near by Arihant and studies in DU. Which is the shortest path for him to reach college?

(ii) What is nearer to Rajghat? Arihant or DU.

4 Draw the same figure at the right hand side on a grid of size 4 cm × 4 cm.

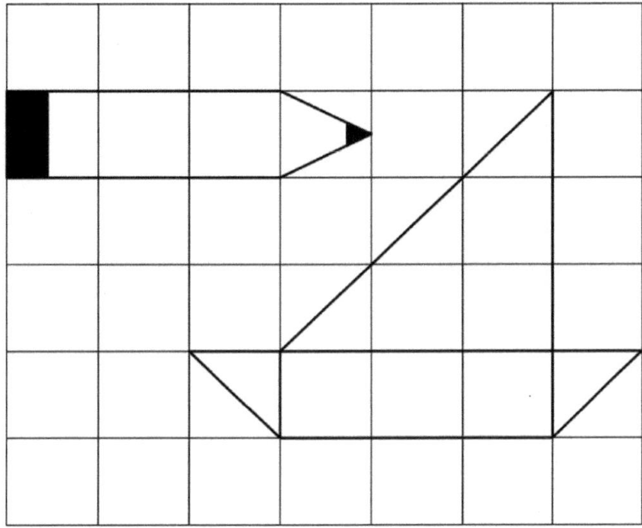

5 The map of 8 towns is given below. Observe the map and answer the following.

[1 cm = 20 km]

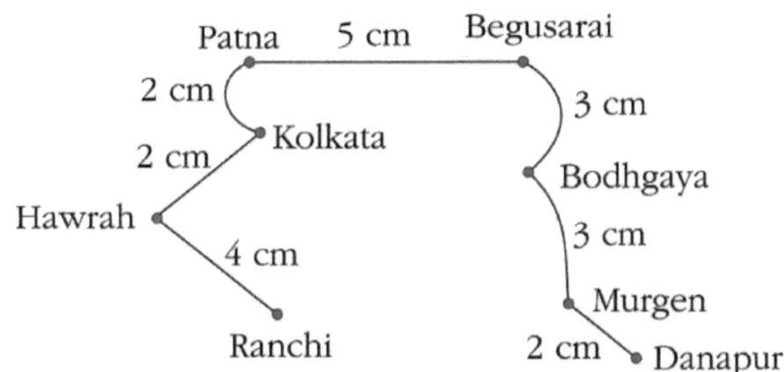

(i) What is the distance (in km) between Ranchi and Kolkata on map?

(ii) Which of the following towns have the shortest road?

(a) Kolkata and Ranchi
(b) Bodhgaya and Murgen
(c) Patna and Begusarai
(d) Howrah and Kolkata

(iii) Which two towns will you cross while coming from Begusarai to Danapur?

(iv) In which direction is Murgen located with respect to Begusarai?

(v) How many kilometres will you have to travel, if you go from Begusarai to Patna?

(vi) Measure the distance (in km) between Danapur and Bodhgaya.

6 **Anuradha's house from the top looks like as shown in the given figure.**

[Scale: 2 cm = 5 m]

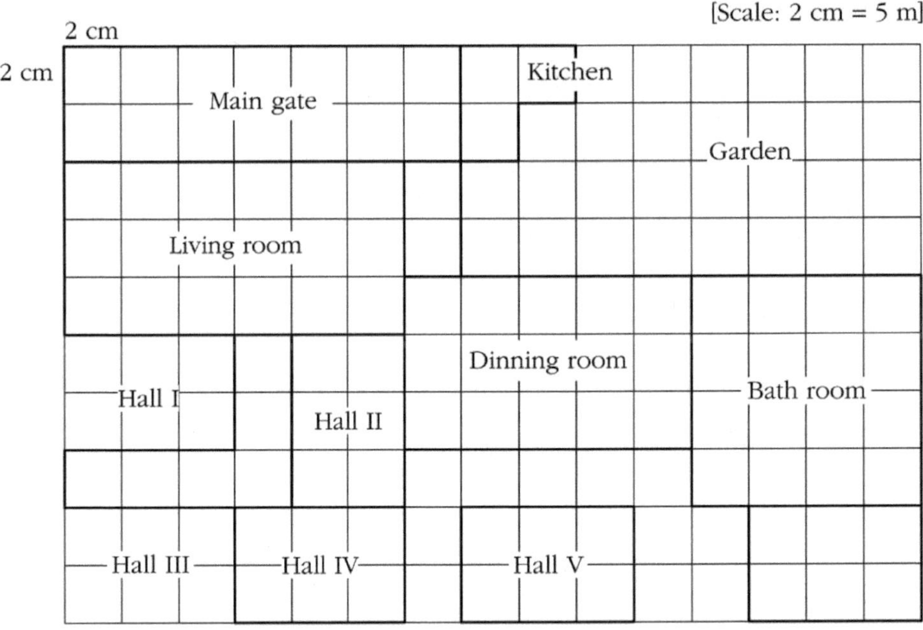

(i) What is the area (in sq cm) of each hall?

(ii) How many times bigger is the area of living room than that of a hall?

(iii) What is the length and width of the dinning room?

(a) Length = 10 cm, width = 6 cm (b) Length = 5 cm, width = 3 cm

(c) Length = 6 cm, width = 6 cm (d) Length = 3 cm, width = 5 cm

(iv) How many times bigger is the area of the dinning room than that of the kitchen?

[Chapter 9]

Boxes and Sketches

1 Identify the 2-D shapes and 3-D shapes.

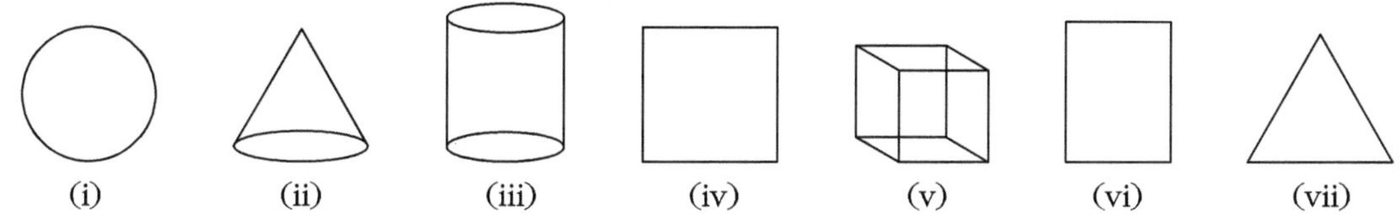

2 Draw the net (in 2-D) of the following things.

Hint The object is a combination of two 3-D shapes.

3 Which of these nets will make a cuboid?

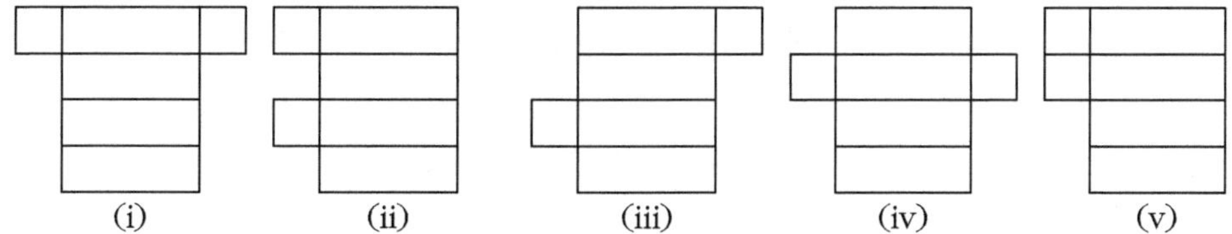

4 Circle the net of the given box which is opened from one side.

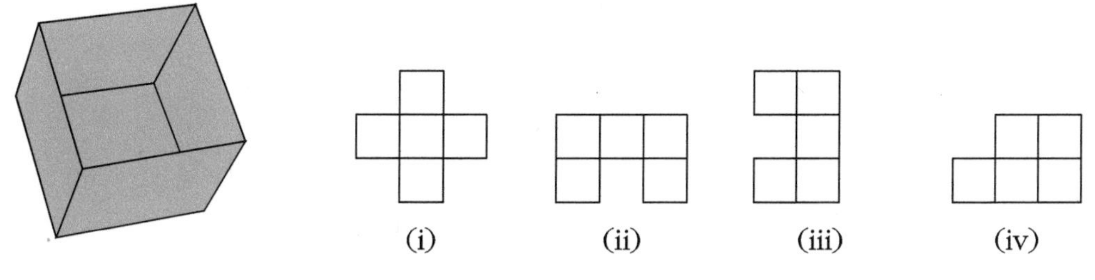

5 Match row I of the shape with the box into which it will fold in row II.

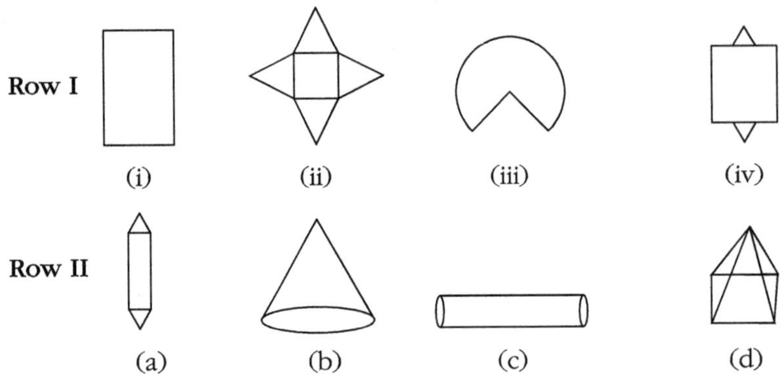

6 Monika drew a floor map of her house as shown below.

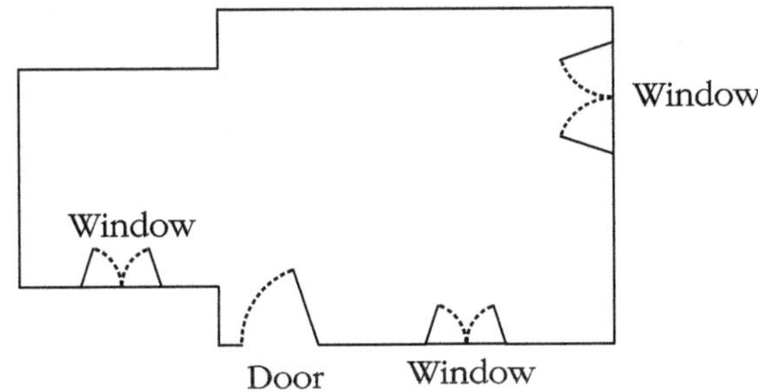

Reena drew deep drawing of Monika's house using the floor map. Circle the correct deep drawing of Monika's house.

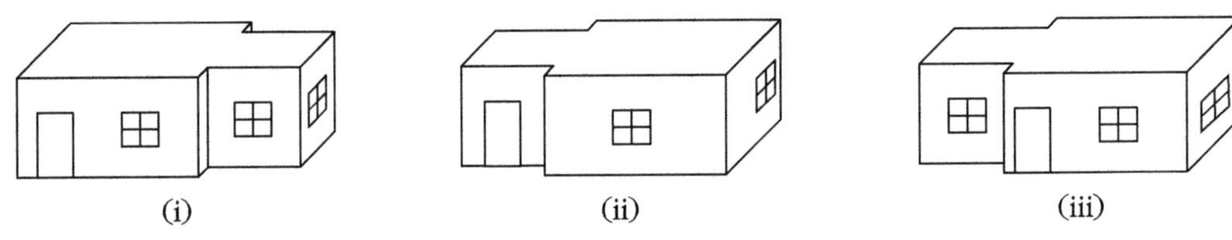

7 This cut-out (net) is folded to make a cube.

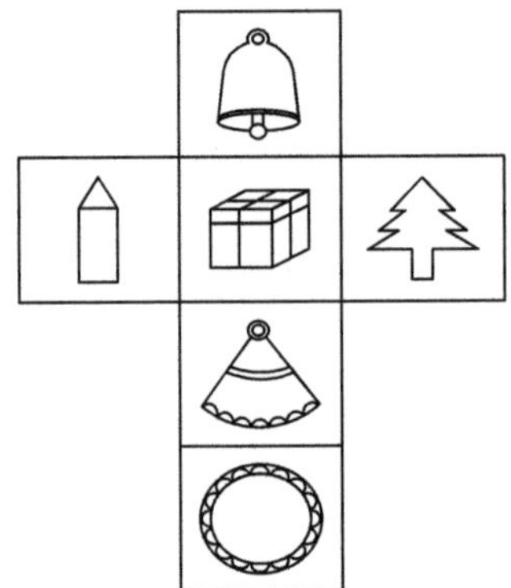

Which of these is the correct deep drawing of that cube?

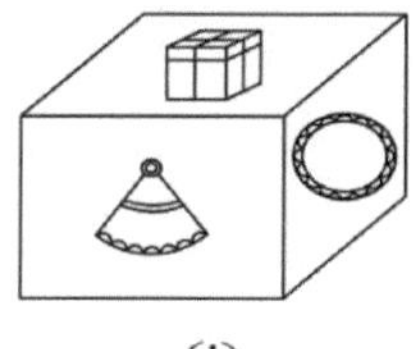
(i)

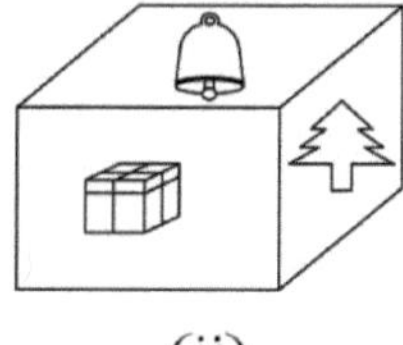
(ii)

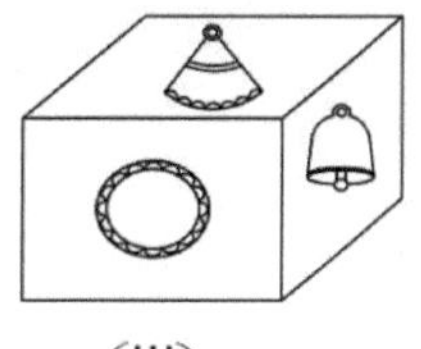
(iii)

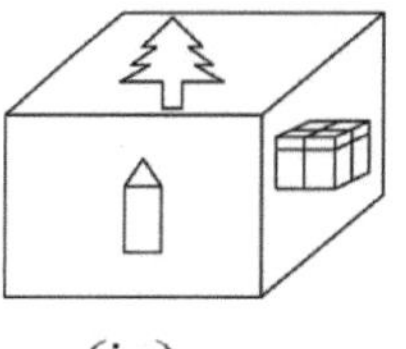
(iv)

8 Draw/Paste the picture of 3 objects which are in a shape of a cube. One has been done for you.

(i) 

(ii) 

(iii) 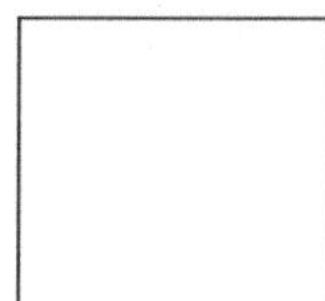

(iv) 

9 Draw/Paste the picture of 3 objects which are in a shape of a cuboid. One has been done for you.

(i) 

(ii) 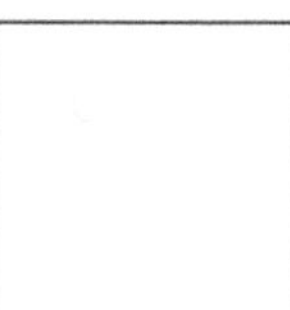

(iii) 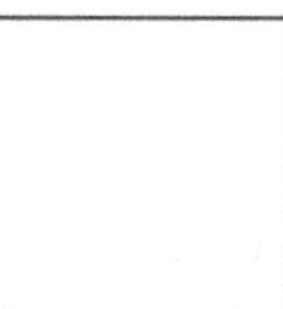

(iv) 

10 Match each net provided in column II to its corresponding object provided in column I.

Column I	Column II
(i) 	(a) 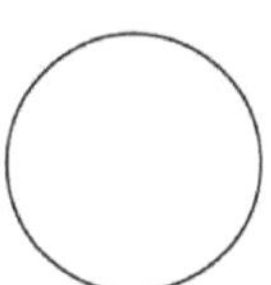

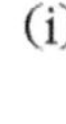

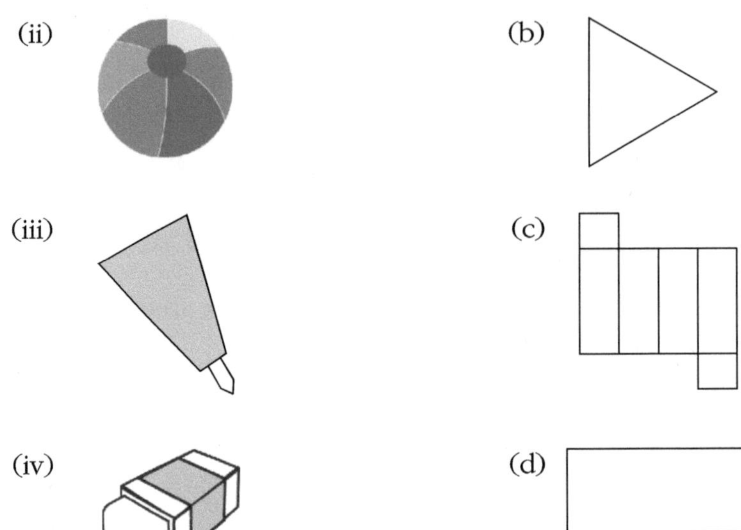

11 Siddharth, Aman and Prerna made this bridge using empty boxes.

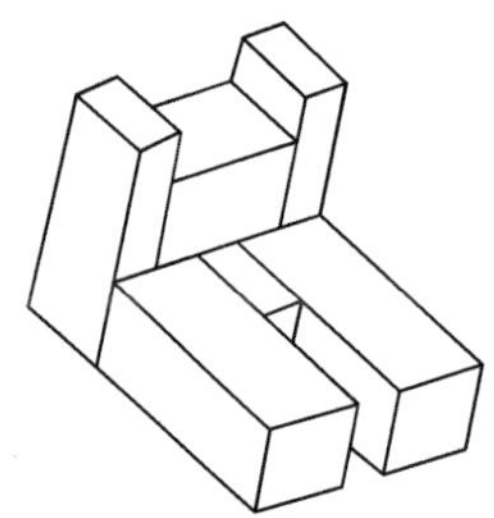

Now, make a drawing to show how this will look.

From the top	From the front	From the side

12 Count the number of cubes used to form the model given in each part.

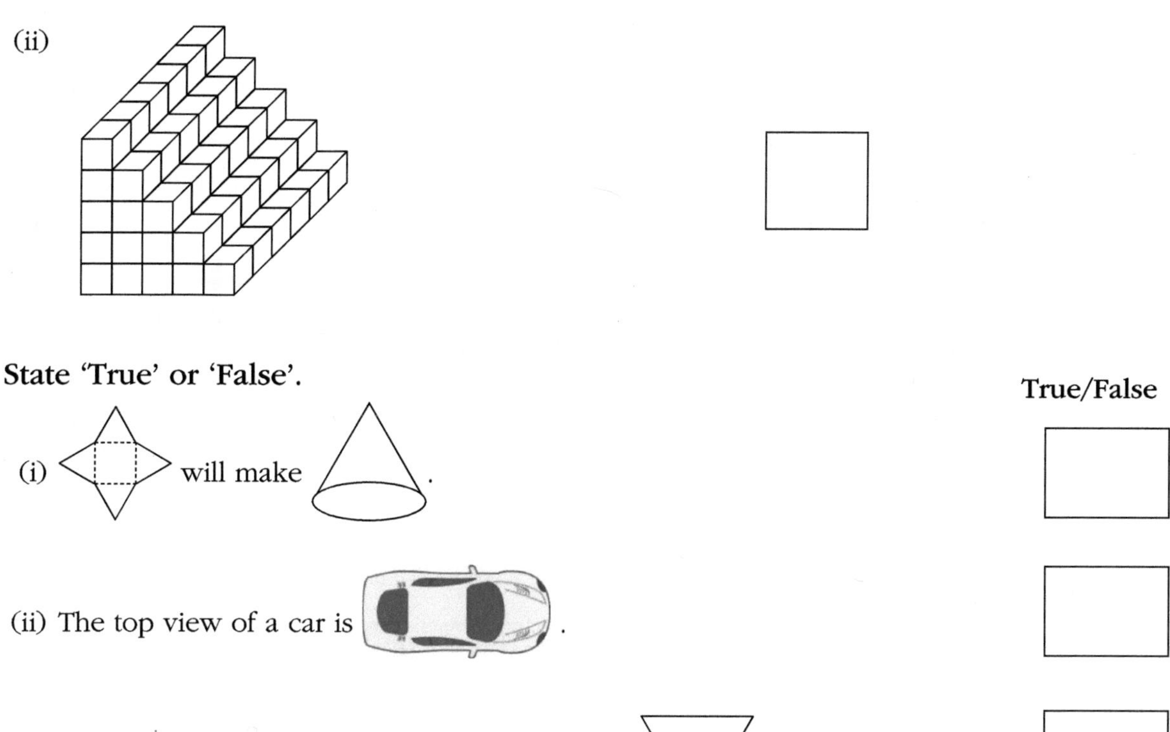

(ii)

13 **State 'True' or 'False'.**

True/False

(i) will make .

(ii) The top view of a car is .

(iii) The net of an ice-cream cone with ice-cream is .

[Chapter 10]

Tenths and Hundredths

1 Measure the length of the following objects using the scale given below. One has been done for you.

(i)

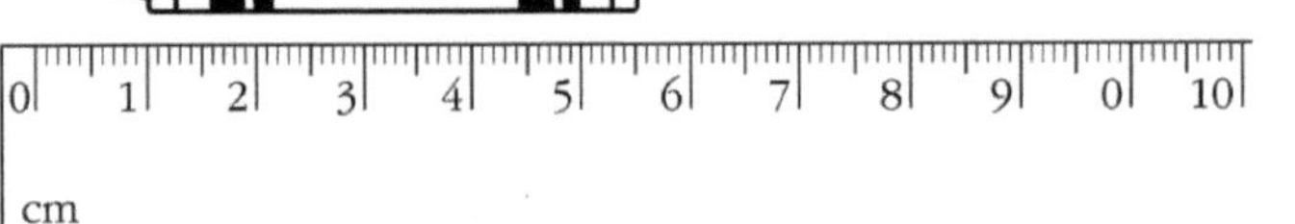

= 5.5 cm

(ii)

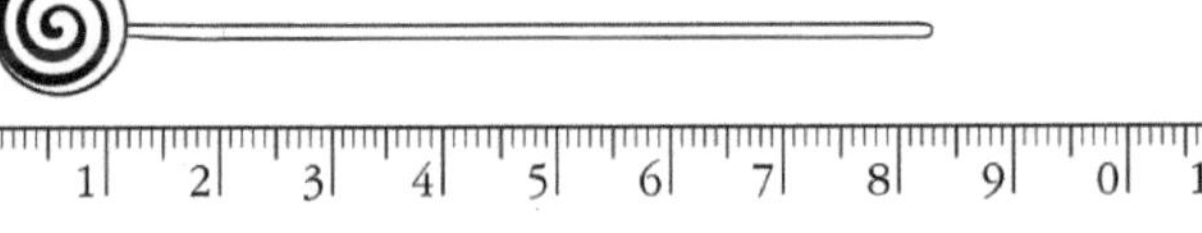

= ________ cm

(iii)

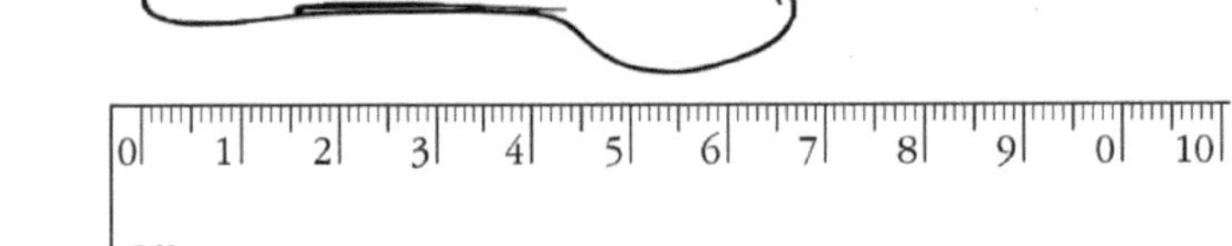

= ________ cm

(iv)

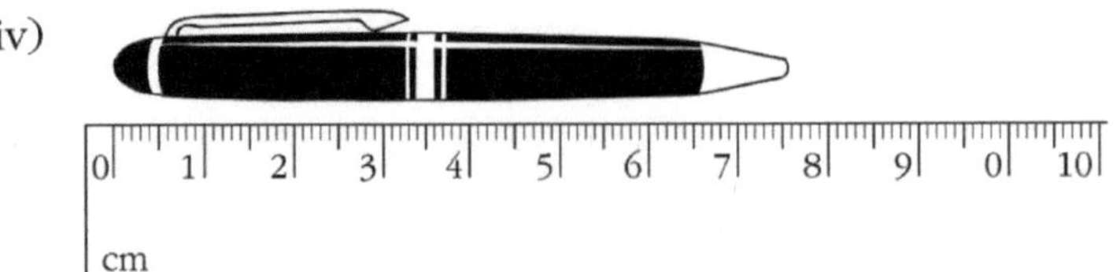

= ________ cm

(v)

= ________ cm

2 If the length of one square block is 1.3 cm, then find the length of the following objects. One has been done for you.

	Objects	Length
(i) 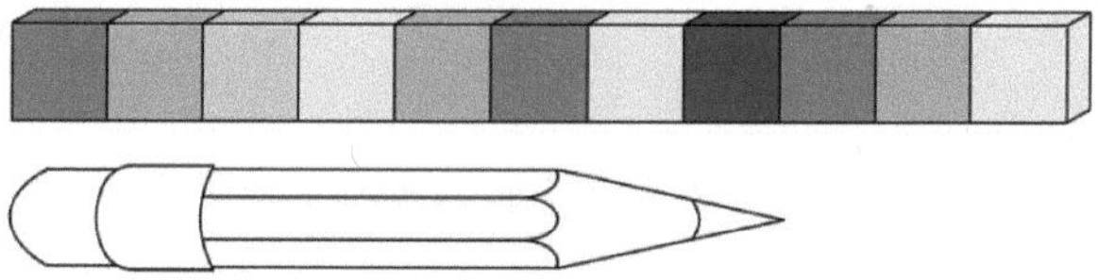		10 cm 4 mm
(ii) 		☐ cm ☐ mm
(iii) 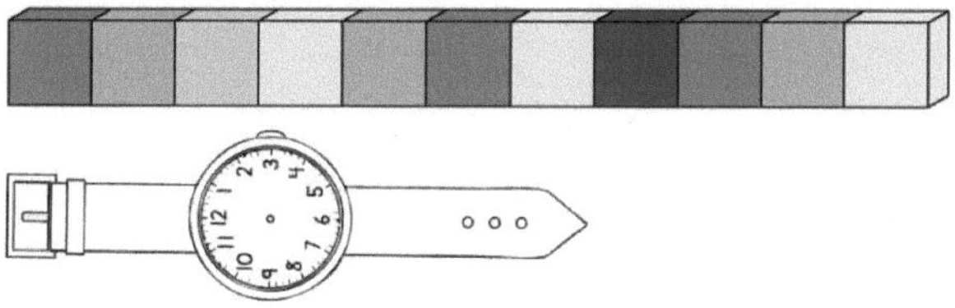		☐ cm ☐ mm
(iv) 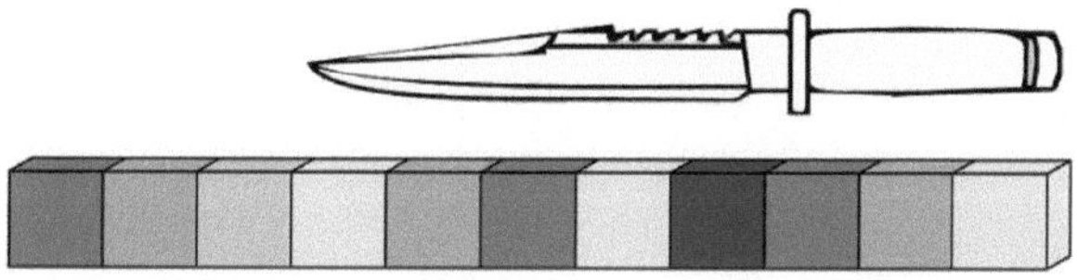		☐ cm ☐ mm
(v) 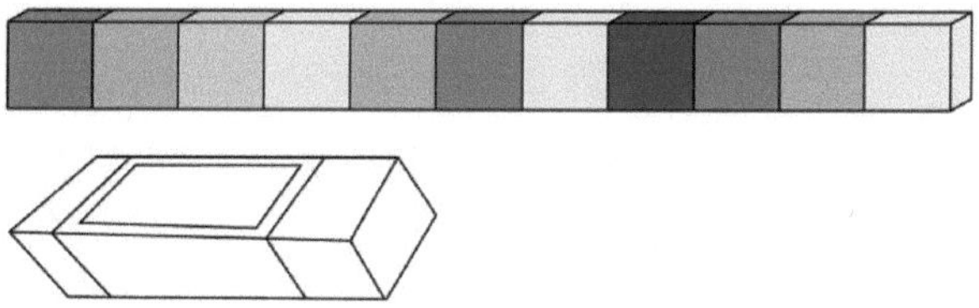		☐ cm ☐ mm

3 Write the following as decimals. One has been done for you.

(i) One tenths = 0.1

(ii) Forty five hundredths = ____________

(iii) Five point three two = ____________

(iv) Six point zero zero one = ____________

(v) 5 tenths and 7 hundredths = ____________

(vi) Thirty two and three tenths = ____________

(vii) Forty six and fifty five hundredths = ____________

4 Solve the following.

(i) 2.53×10 = ____________ (ii) 3.25×100 = ____________

(iii) $\frac{32}{10}$ = ____________ (iv) $\frac{46}{100}$ = ____________

(v) 0.76×100 = ____________ (vi) $73.25 \div 100$ = ____________

(vii) 63.75×100 = ____________

5 Match the following columns.

	Column I		Column II
(i)	0.5×0.1	(a)	0.55
(ii)	$13 \div 100$	(b)	0.13
(iii)	$2.5 - 2.25$	(c)	0.5
(iv)	10×0.05	(d)	0.25
(v)	$0.5 + 0.05$	(e)	0.05

6 Use the correct sign $<$, $=$ or $>$ in below questions.

(i) 6.43 ☐ 6.34 (ii) 2.87 ☐ 2.32 + 0.55

(iii) 5.21 ☐ 5.12 (iv) 3.189 ☐ 3.098

7 Convert each of the following according to the given instruction.

(i) 25 mm into cm (ii) 25 cm into m

(iii) 252 paise into rupees (iv) 2550 paise into rupees

(v) 720 cm into m (vi) 0.25 m into cm

(vii) ₹ 8.4 into paise

8 Write the correct decimal represented by the shaded part of given design. One has been done for you.

(i) 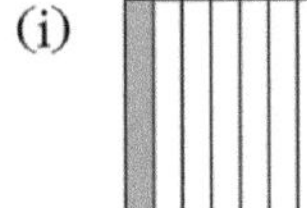 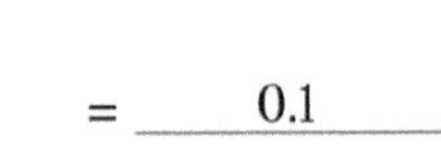 = 0.1

(ii) 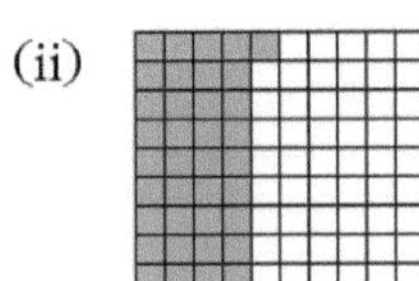 = ____________

(iii) 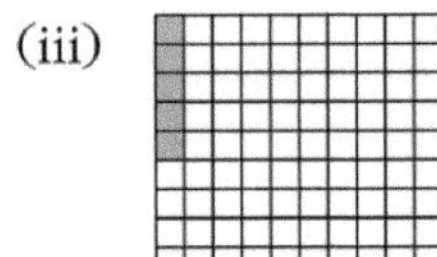 = ____________

(iv) 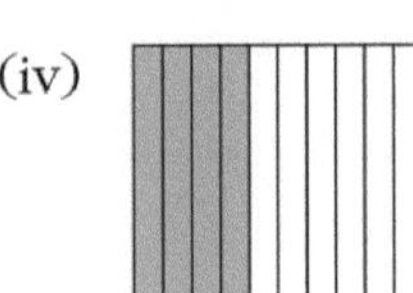 = ____________

9 Match the following columns. One has been done for you.

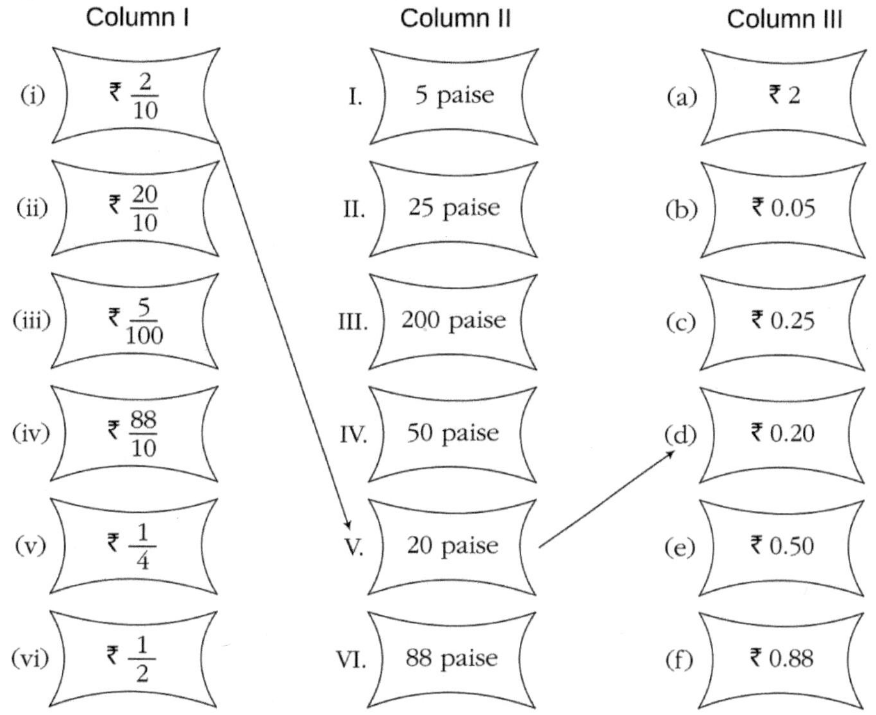

10 Write the decimal number.

(i) $1 + \frac{3}{10} + \frac{5}{100}$ = ____________

(ii) $20 + 6 + \frac{40}{100}$ = ____________

(iii) $200 + 0 + 2 + \frac{1}{10} + \frac{3}{100}$ = ____________

(iv) $50 + 6 + \frac{0}{10} + \frac{0}{100}$ = ____________

(v) $70 + 5 + \frac{6}{10} + \frac{0}{100}$ = ____________

(vi) $2 + \frac{0}{10} + \frac{5}{100}$ = ____________

11 Word problems.

(i) Raju went to a shop to purchase a pen, two pencils and five erasers. The cost of a pen is ₹ 2.50, a pencil is ₹ 2 and an eraser is ₹ 0.75. How much did he pay to the shopkeeper?

____

____

(ii) Monika paid ₹ 8.25 for chips and ₹ 5.75 for chocolates. She got ₹ 7 as return from the shopkeeper. How much money did she pay?

____

____

(iii) Rani ran in the race and covered the distance in 16.5 s, Priya covered it in 15.9 s and Sonia covered it in 14.7 s. Who is the winner?

(iv) In Class V of DPS Delhi, the height of a student Ravi is 1.5 m and it is 0.15 m more than his height in Class IV. Find the height of Ravi in Class IV. Also, if Mona's height is 1.5 times that of Ravi, then find the height of Mona.

(v) Rohit had ₹ 150. He bought sugar for ₹ 19.50, rice for ₹ 90 and biscuits for ₹ 28.25. How much money was he left with?

(vi) The temperature on Wednesday was 38.5°C and is increased by 1.7°C on Thursday. Find the temperature on Thursday.

12 Price list of items in a shop is given below

Item	**Quantity**	**Cost** (in ₹)
Chocolates	2	15.25
Balloons	6	18.06
Chips packets	8	100.50
Paper cups	10	2.50
Napkins	1 box	31.50

Based on the above price list, complete the table given below.

	Item		Cost (in ₹)
(i)	2 chocolates and 4 chips packets	=	________
(ii)	15 paper cups and 4 balloons	=	________
(iii)	2 boxes of napkins, 3 balloons and 2 chocolates	=	________

13 The following table shows the value of money from different countries in Indian rupees.

Country	**Money**	**Value** (in ₹)
US	U S dollors	65.9
Austria	Euros	73.48
England	Pounds	101.03
Singapore	Singapore dollors	46.35
Japan	Yen	0.55
China	Yuan	10.33

Answer the questions given below on the basis of the above table.

(i) Which country is money cost the least in Indian rupees?

____

____

____

____

(ii) Ruchi's friend works in England. She earns 300 pounds as salary. Rahul's friend works in US and gets 400 dollars as salary. Who gets more salary in rupees and by how much?

____

____

____

____

(iii) Shreya's aunt who lives in Austria send her 50 euros every month. Shreya uses ₹ 2700 every month and saves the rest. How much money (in ₹) does Shreya save every month?

(iv) Ishita wants to exchange some money (in ₹) for yen. How many yen can she get for ₹ 275?

14 The following map shows the amount of rainfall received in various states in India during July 2016.

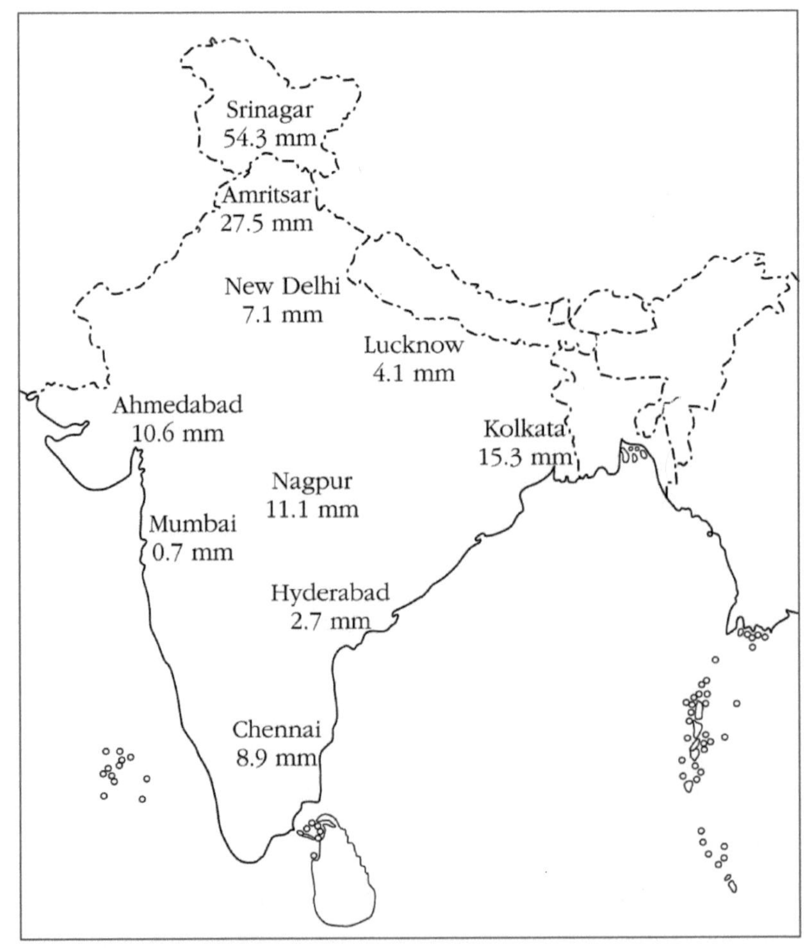

Answer the following questions on the basis of above map.

(i) Which place had received the highest rainfall in July?

(ii) How humid is Srinagar compared to New Delhi?

(iii) How much more rainfall is needed in Kolkata to reach 20 mm?

(iv) How much less rainfall is received in Ahmedabad than that in Amritsar?

15 The following table shows various substance and the temperature at which it starts boiling.

Substance	**Temperature at which it starts boiling**
Water	100° C
Gold	2843.69° C
Silver	143.27° C
Copper	125.98° C

Now, answer the following questions on the basis of above table ______.

(i) Which substance has maximum temperature of boiling?

(ii) What is the difference between the boiling temperatures of gold and silver?

(iii) Which substance has minimum temperature of boiling?

(iv) What is the difference between the maximum and minimum temperatures?

[Chapter **11**]

Area and its Boundary

1 **A square postal stamp** (3 cm × 3 cm) **has an area of 9 sq cm.**

I. Determine the area and perimeter of the following rectangles on the basis of it.

(i)

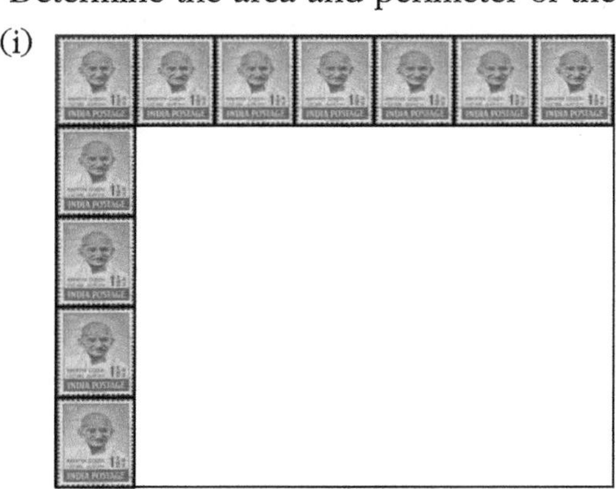

Area = ____________ sq cm

Perimeter = ____________ cm

(ii)

Area = ____________ sq cm

Perimeter = ____________ cm

II. How many postal stamps are needed to cover the following rectangles?

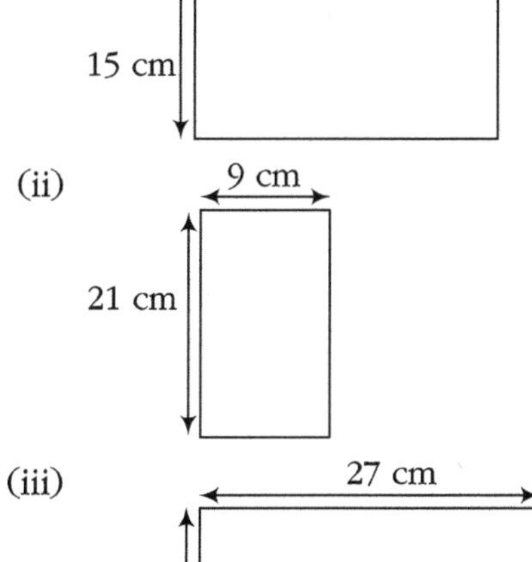

(i) = ____________________

(ii) = ____________________

(iii) 27 cm × 24 cm = ____________________

2 Complete the table given below.

	Length	**Breadth**	**Perimeter**	**Area** (in sq cm/m)
(i)	4 m	3 m	______	12
(ii)	3 cm	3 cm	______	______
(iii)	30 m	______	110 m	750
(iv)	20 m	12 m	______	______
(v)	10 cm	8 cm	______	______
(vi)	______	11 cm	44 cm	______

3 Divide the following grid into equal parts.

(i)

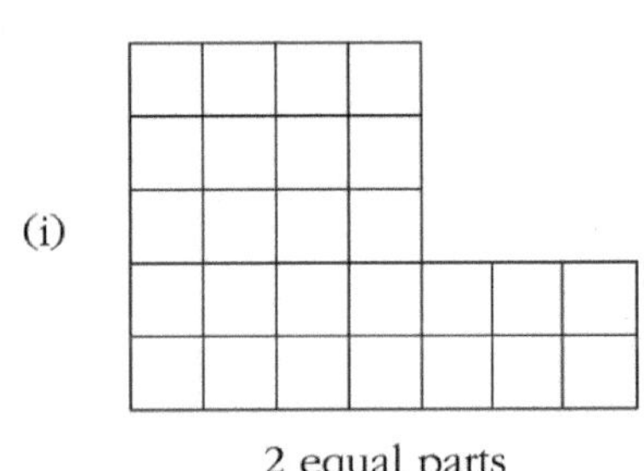

2 equal parts

(ii)

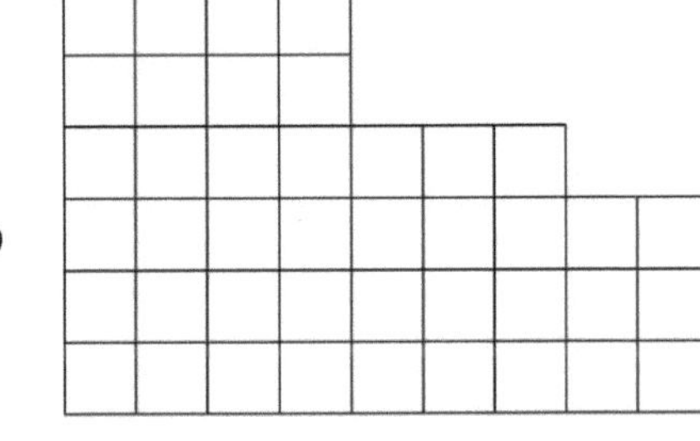

3 equal parts

4 Find the perimeter and area of the given square and rectangle and fill in the blanks.

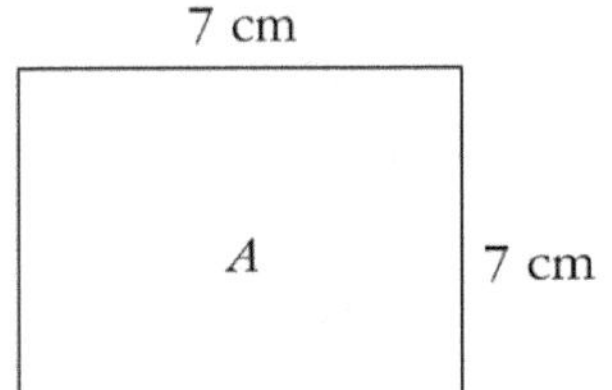

16 cm

B

6 cm

(i) Area of figure *A* = ______________________

(ii) Area of figure *B* = ______________________

(iii) Perimeter of figure *A* = ______________________

(iv) Perimeter of figure *B* = ______________________

(v) Area of figure *B* is __________ more than area of figure *A*.

(vi) Perimeter of figure *B* is __________ more than perimeter of figure *A*.

5 Find the perimeter and area of shaded part of given figures.

(i)

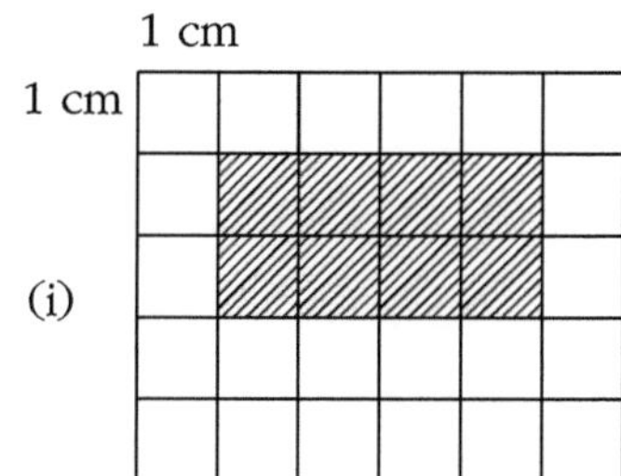

(ii)

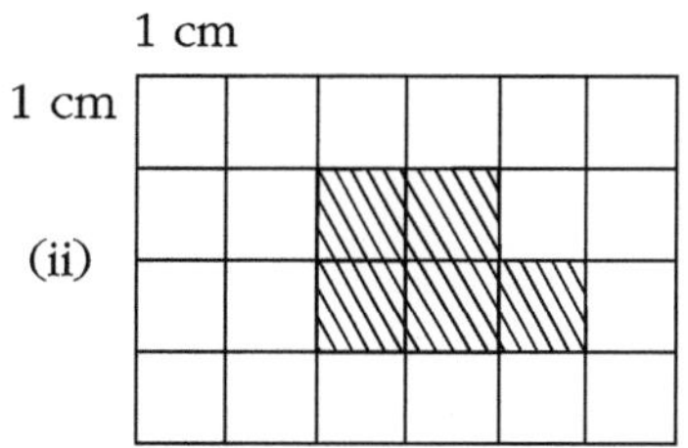

(iii)

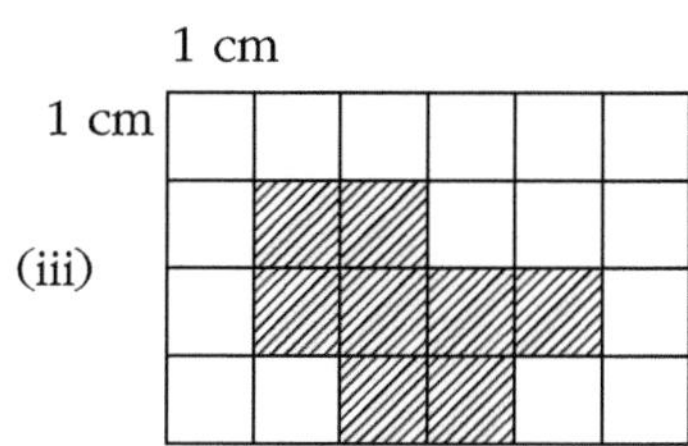

(iv)

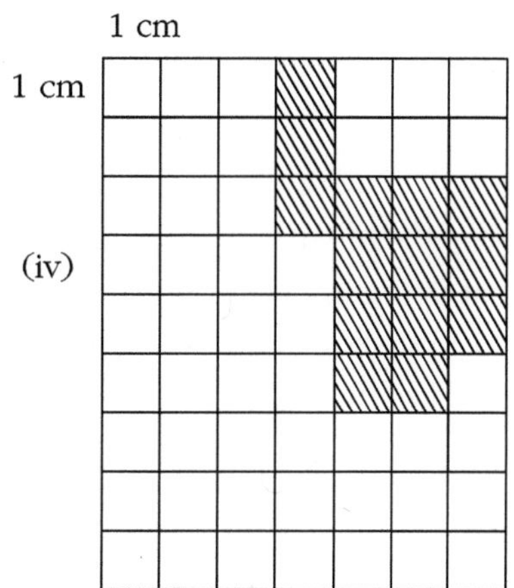

6 Find the perimeter of the given figures.

(i)

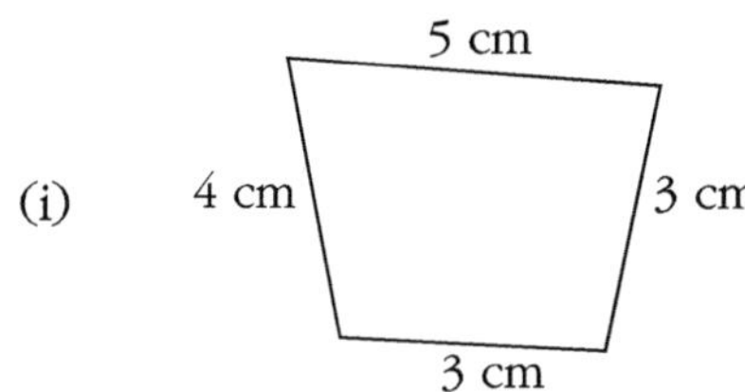

= ____________________

(ii)

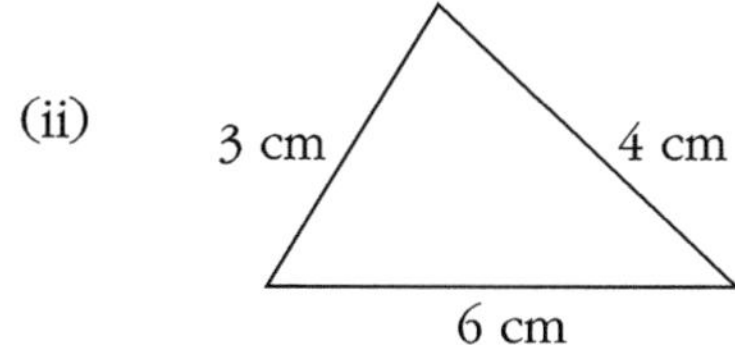

= ____________________

(iii)

5 cm
2 cm 2 cm
1 cm 1 cm
3 cm 3 cm
3 cm

= ____________________

(iv)

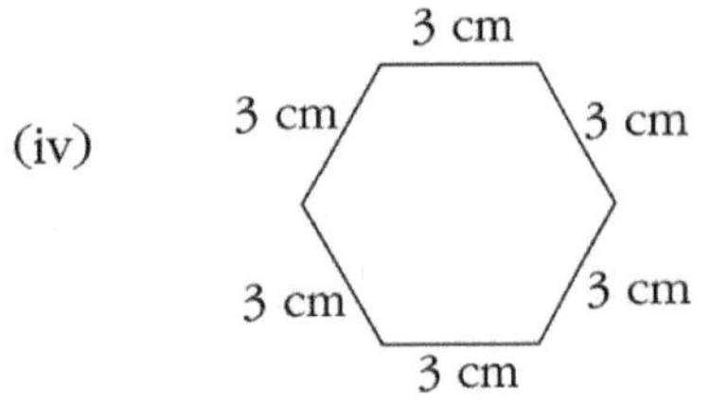

= ____________________

(v)

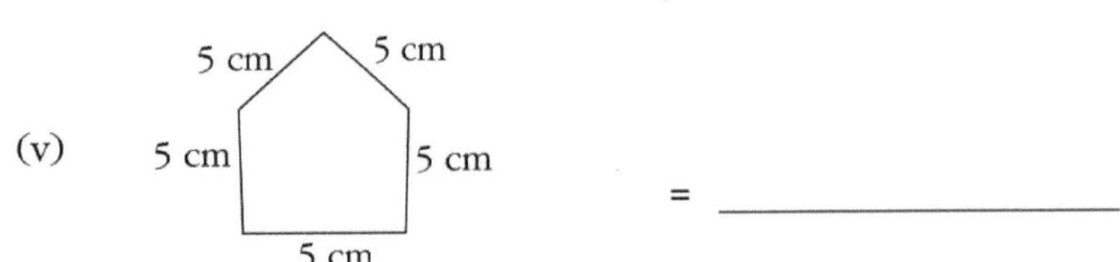

= ____________________

7 Multiple choice questions.

(i) What is the area of a square sheet, if its one side is 16 cm long?

(a) 196 sq m (b) 256 sq m

(c) 324 sq m (d) 32 sq m

(ii) A rectangular plot is 25 m × 15 m in dimensions. The total wire needed to fence around it is

(a) 375 sq m (b) 80 sq m

(c) 40 sq m (d) 300 sq m

(iii) Which has greater area, if a square of side 10 cm or a rectangle of dimensions 5 cm × 4 cm?

(a) Square (b) Rectangle

(c) Both are equal (d) Can't say

(iv) If a square sheet has perimeter of 72 cm, then what is its area?

(a) 72 sq cm (b) 36 sq cm

(c) 180 sq cm (d) 324 sq cm

8 Word problems.

(i) The following figure shows Ram's garden.

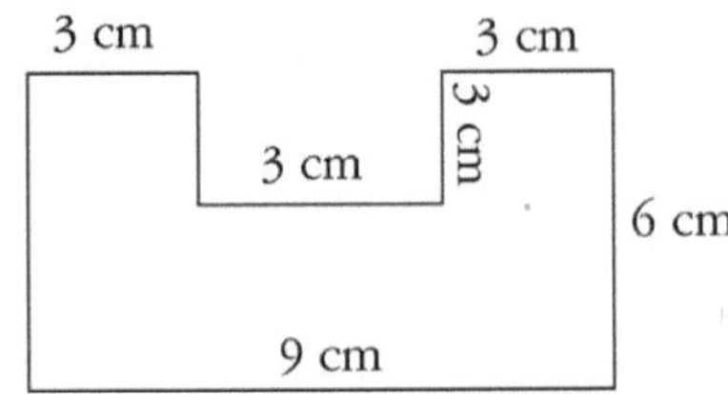

He wants to fence it with a wire to avoid animals from coming in the garden. Find the length of wire required to fence the boundary.

(ii) A school ground has dimensions of 24 m × 36 m. In the school assembly, teachers made the students sit on the ground. If one student occupies 2 m × 3 m of space, then how many students can sit on the ground?

(iii) A solar panel is of rectangular shape. Its dimension is 4 m × 3 m. A frame needs to be built around the panel. What length of the frame is required?

(iv) Consider the following figure about a room and answer the following questions.

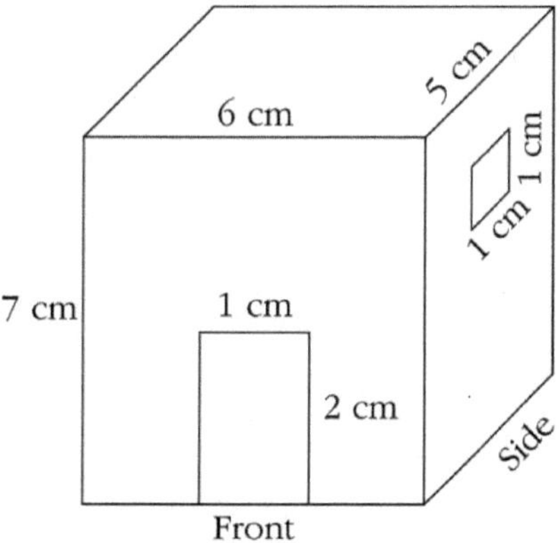

(a) Find the area of side wall. (Excluding window)

(b) Find the area of front wall. (Excluding door)

(v) Sneha wants to paint the shaded portion of the wall as shown below

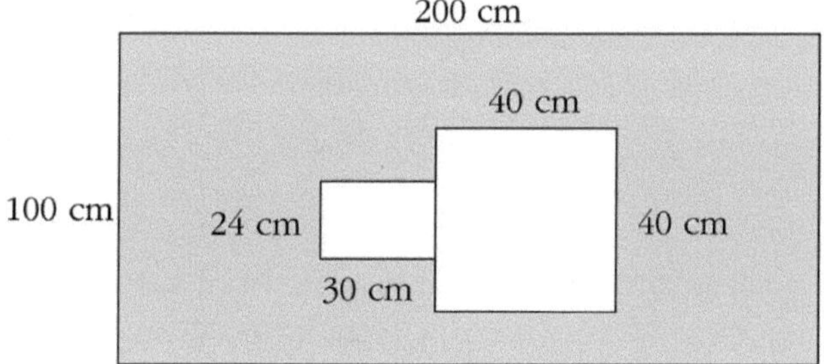

What is the area of the wall she wants to paint?

(vi) Ramdhar had 200 m fencing wire to fence his field. What is the maximum area, he can fence with one side of 50 m?

50 m

9 **I. Ankur tried to make different rectangles (with a ribbon) having an area of 1600 sq m. Fill in the blanks to write the length of ribbon required in each case.**

(i)

20 m × 80 m

Ribbon required for (i) = ________ m

(ii)

160 m × 10 m

Ribbon required for (ii) = ________ m

(iii)

1600 m × 1 m

Ribbon required for (iii) = ________ m

(iv)

16000 m × 0.1 m

Ribbon required for (iv) = ________ m

II. For which part is the maximum length of ribbon required?

10 Nine squares with side lengths 1, 4, 7, 8, 9, 10, 14, 15 and 18 cm can be fitted together with no gaps and no overlaps to form a rectangle. What are the dimensions of that rectangle? Also, find its perimeter and area.

Chapter **12**

Smart Charts

1 The number of fruit juice packs sold in a school canteen in a week are given below

One → |, Two → ⌐, Three → ⊓, Four → □, Five → ⊠

Now, answer the following questions on the basis of above information.

(i) Fill in the numbers using tally marks. One has been done for you.

	Fruit	Tally marks	Number
(a)	Apple		18
(b)	Orange		________
(c)	Pinneapple		________
(d)	Guava		________
(e)	Litchi		________
(f)	Mixed fruit		________

(ii) Find the total number of packs sold in the week. __________

(iii) Which juice is preferred by most number of children? __________

(iv) Pineapple juice is consumed thrice as much as Guava? (True/False) __________

(v) Least favourite juice is __________ .

(vi) The number of Guava packs sold were __________ less than the number of apple packs sold.

2 Shrishti has a habit of plucking flowers from her uncle's garden. The following data shows the number of flowers she plucked from Monday to Friday. Draw a tally chart to represent the data. One has been done for you.

Day	Monday	Tuesday	Wednesday	Thursday	Friday
Number of flowers	20	14	16	19	30

Flower Plucking

Day	Number of flowers
Monday	
Tuesday	
Wednesday	⊠ ⊠ ⊠ |
Thursday	
Friday	

3 In an activity class, the teacher asked children about their favourite sport. The teacher collected the answer and made a table as shown below

Sport	Number of children
Cricket	35
Badminton	17
Football	40
Volleyball	—
Basketball	17
Table tennis	3
Total children in the activity class	120

Find the missing number.

4 A pictograph is given below based on favourite winter sports of few children.

Favourite Winter Sports

Luge	✳✳✳✳✳✳✳✳
Bobsledding	✳✳
Ski jumping	✳✳✳✳✳✳✳

✳ = 2 children

(i) Use the data in the pictograph to complete the following tally chart.

Favourite Winter Sports

Sport	Number of children
Luge	________
Bobsledding	________
Ski jumping	________

(ii) Answer the following questions on the basis of given pictograph.

(a) Which winter sport is the least favourite among the children?

(b) Which sport is most liked by the children?

(c) How many more children like luge than bobsledding?

5 **100 children were asked which kind of cartoons were their favourite. Their replies are collected in the table given below.**

Coin	Number
Ben 10	36
Spider man	28
Tom & Jerry	20
Doremon	16

She draw a chapati chart to show this. Fill her chapati chart on the basis of above information.

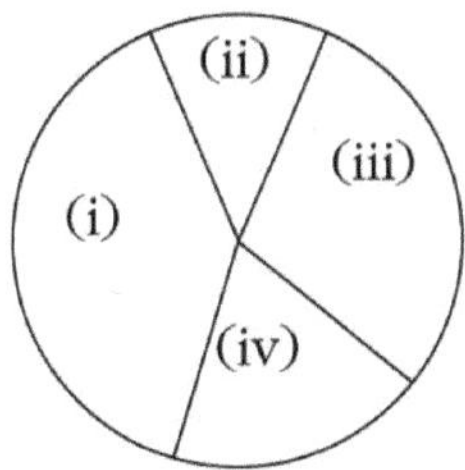

6 **A group of children went to zoo. They saw different types of animals. Teacher asked them which animal did they like? On the basis of their answers, she made a graph. Use the following graph and answer the questions given below.**

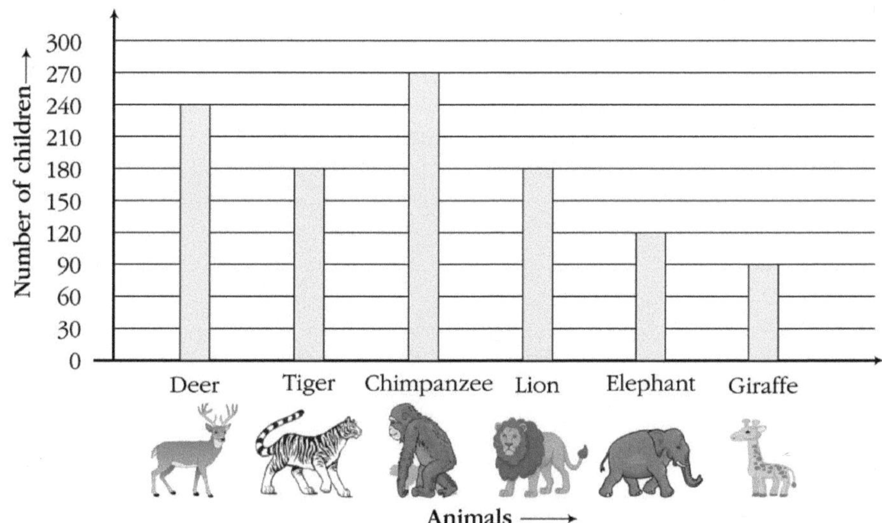

(i) Write a number at the top of each bar to display the number of children who liked each animal.

(ii) More number of children like tiger than elephant. (True/False) ________

(iii) Which animal is liked by double the number of children who like Giraffe? ________

(iv) How many more children like lion than elephant? ________

7 Jany has collected a data of different creatures in her garden. Draw a bar chart to represent the data. One has been done for you.

Ladybug	Grasshopper	Dragonfly	Butterfly
7	3	5	9

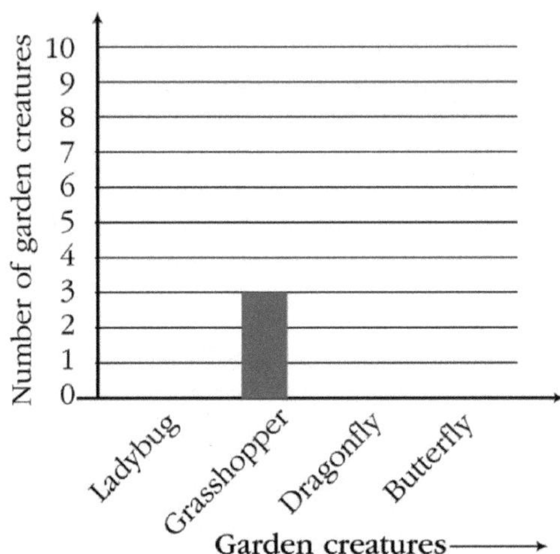

8 Use the table given below and answer the questions.

The following table shows the number of Mathematics books published by Arihant increases every year.

Time	Number of books
Start	7
1 year	16
2 year	35
3 year	75
4 year	160
5 year	350
6 year	—
7 year	—

(i) After each year the number of books published was

(a) a little less than double the number of books published in the last year

(b) double the number in the last year

(c) a little more than double the number in the last year

(d) 2 less than the number in the last year

(ii) At the end of year 6, the number of books published was closed to

(a) 400 (b) 600 (c) 800

(iii) After which year did the number of books publish cross 1400?

9 **Suchi went to a wedding along with her parents. She couldn't recognise each one so her father made a family tree.**

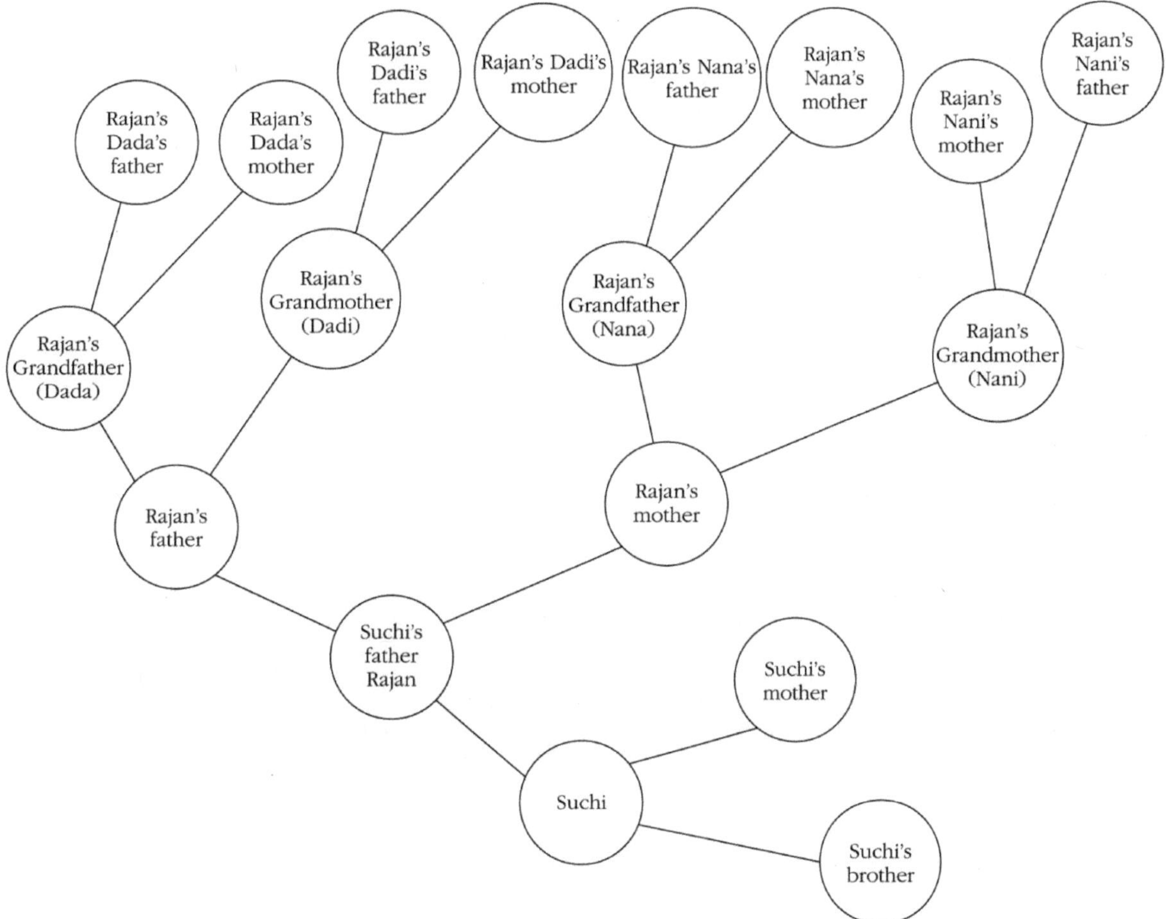

Answer the following questions on the basis of above family tree.

(i) How many grandparents in all does Rajan have? ________

(ii) How many paternal grandparents in all does Suchi have? ________

10 Tushar kept record of how long it took to finish his homework each day?

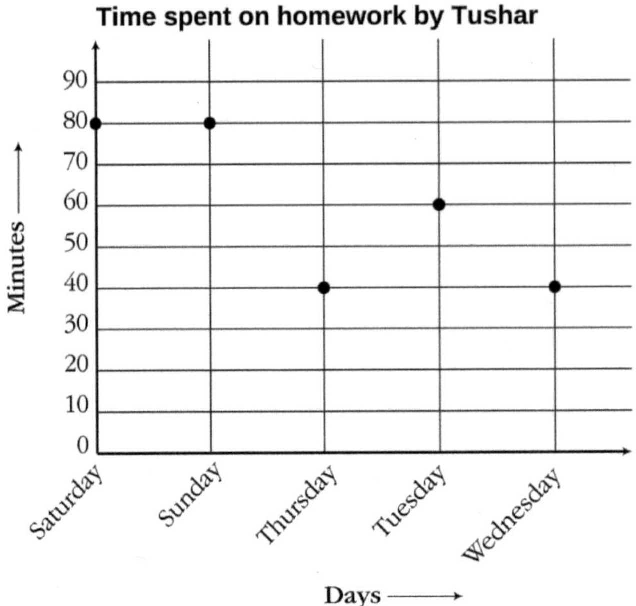

Answer the following questions on the basis of above graph.

(i) How long did Tushar take to finish his homework on Wednesday?

____

____

(ii) On which day(s) did Tushar take the maximum time to finish his homework?

____

____

(iii) Tushar took the same time to finish his homework on Saturday and Sunday. (True/False)

____

____

(iv) Tushar took 20 more minutes to complete his homework on Thursday than on Wednesday. Represent it in a new graph by using dot mark as above.

[Chapter **13**]

Ways to Multiply and Divide

1 Multiplication — (Two digit numbers)

Fill in the blank spaces.

(i) 32×21

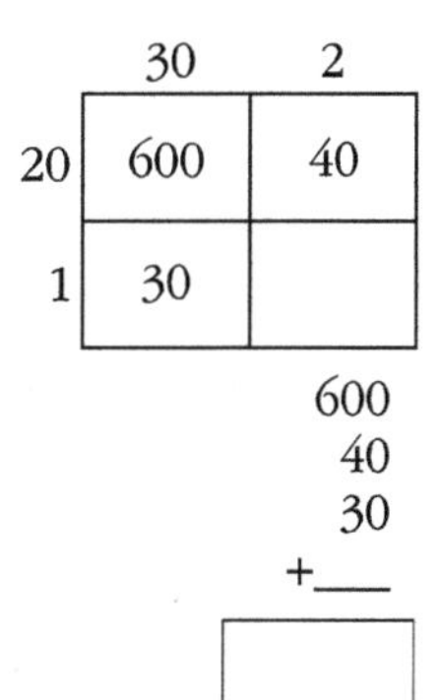

(ii) 54×26

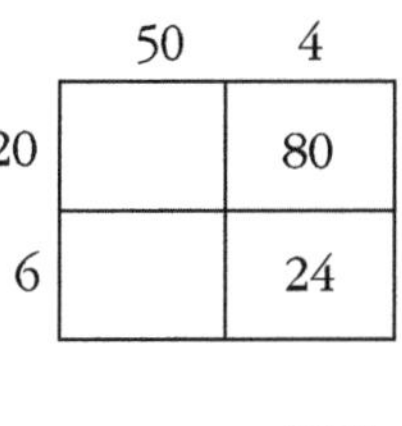

(iii) 54×38

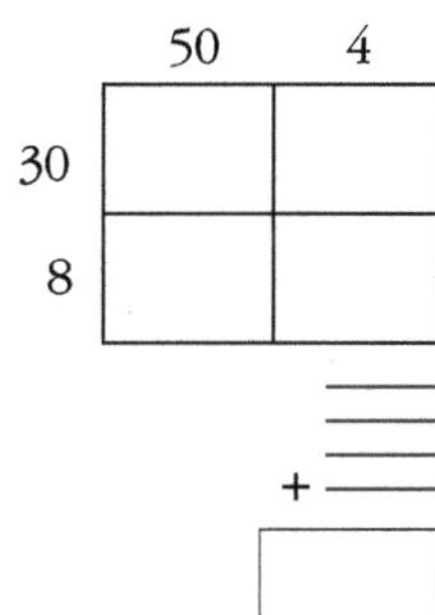

(iv) 27×56

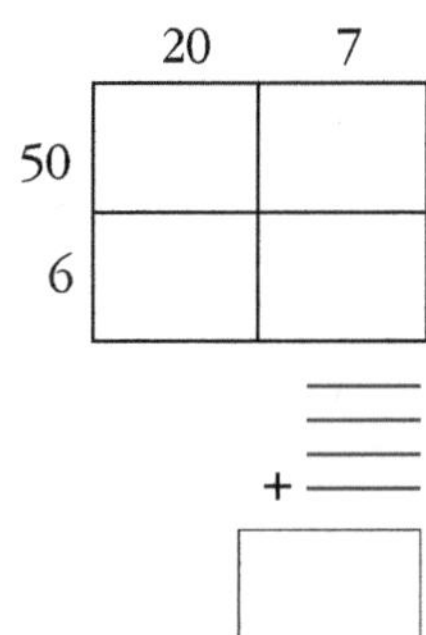

2 Multiply and then round off to nearest 100. One has been done for you.

(i)

456
× 14

Product 6384

Nearest 100 6400

(ii)

526
× 16

Product

Nearest 100

(iii)

$$\begin{array}{r} 854 \\ \times\ 13 \end{array}$$

Product ☐

Nearest 100 ☐

(iv)

$$\begin{array}{r} 132 \\ \times\ 164 \end{array}$$

Product ☐

Nearest 100 ☐

3 Ram bought three pieces of the cloth as shown below

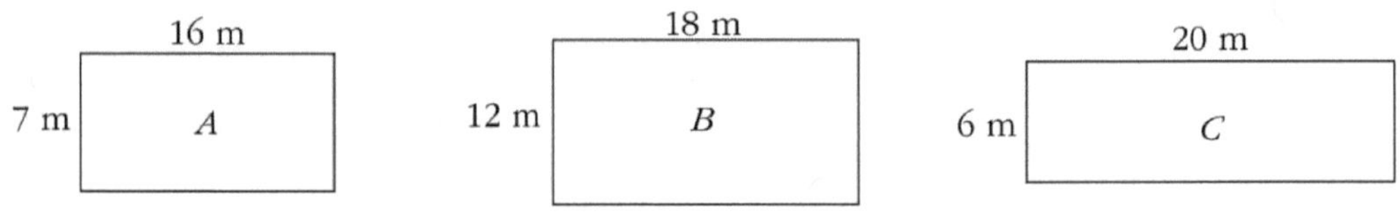

Cloth	Length	Breadth
A	16 m	7 m
B	18 m	12 m
C	20 m	6 m

Answer the following questions on the basis of above.

(i) What is the total square metres of cloth of each type bought by Ram?

Cloth *A* = ____________________ square metre

Cloth *B* = ____________________ square metre

Cloth *C* = ____________________ square metre

(ii) He bought cloth *A* at the rate of ₹ 70 for a square metre, cloth *B* at ₹ 95 for a square metre and cloth *C* at ₹ 120 for a square metre. What is the total cost of all the three clothes?

____

____

4 **Radha's mother took a loan of ₹ 14000. Radha needs to pay it back by giving ₹ 1000 every month. So, she started working in a factory for ₹ 40 per day.**

(i) How much will she earn in one month?

____

____

(ii) Does she earn enough to help pay the loan every month?

____

____

(iii) How much will she earn in an year? (Take only 30 days in every month)

____

____

5 **Answer the following questions.**

(i) Shailendra works in a factory. He is paid ₹ 102 for one day work. If he works for 61 days, then how much will he earn?

(ii) Harish took a loan to build his house. He has to pay back ₹ 325 every month for 3 years. How much will he pay back in 3 years?

(iii) A milk vendor sells 1 litre of milk for ₹ 23. In one month, he sells 320 litres of milk. How much does he earn in a month?

6 **Fun with multiplication.**

Each letter *a*, *b* and *c* here stands for *a* number.

$$\begin{array}{r} a\ a\ a \\ \times\ a\ a\ a \\ \hline a\ a\ a \\ a\ a\ a\ 0 \\ a\ a\ a\ 0\ 0 \\ \hline a\ b\ c\ b\ a \\ \hline \end{array}$$

If $a = 1$, then what are the values of *b* and *c*?

7 **Divide.**

(i) $4\overline{)4764}($ (ii) $3\overline{)3945}($

(iii) $8\overline{)2576}($ (iv) $9\overline{)7209}($

(v) $3\overline{)4320}($ (vi) $15\overline{)5280}($

(vii) $17\overline{)4913}($ (viii) $21\overline{)9576}($

8 **Do the following divisions. Also, check your results by multiplication.**

(i) $769 \div 9$ (ii) $768 \div 6$

(iii) $470 \div 7$ (iv) $900 \div 10$

(v) $4720 \div 14$ (vi) $738 \div 5$

9 **Tick (✓) the best story problem.**

Each line gives a story. You have to choose the question which makes the best story problem. One has been done for you.

(i) Rama wants 70 rose flowers. One flower costs ₹ 12.

(a) How many flowers did Rama buy? ☐

(b) How much money did Rama pay? ☑

(c) How much money is Rama left with? ☐

(ii) 764 children went to a picnic. Each bus can carry 48 children.

(a) How many children did each bus carry? ☐

(b) How many children went for picnic? ☐

(c) How many buses do they need? ☐

(iii) A shopkeeper has 404 articles to sell. One article costs ₹ 10.

(a) How many articles will the shopkeeper buy? ☐

(b) How much money will the shopkeeper earns? ☐

(c) How much money will the shopkeeper left with? ☐

(iv) Jassy bought 46 pencils. Cost of one pencil is ₹ 5.

(a) How many pencils did Jassy buy? ☐

(b) What is the cost of 5 pencils? ☐

(c) How much money does she pay for the pencils? ☐

10 **Frame a word problem on the basis of given clues.**

(i) Clue : $9750 \div 15$ (money got by each student)

____

____

(ii) Clue : 225×30 (salary earned in a month)

____

____

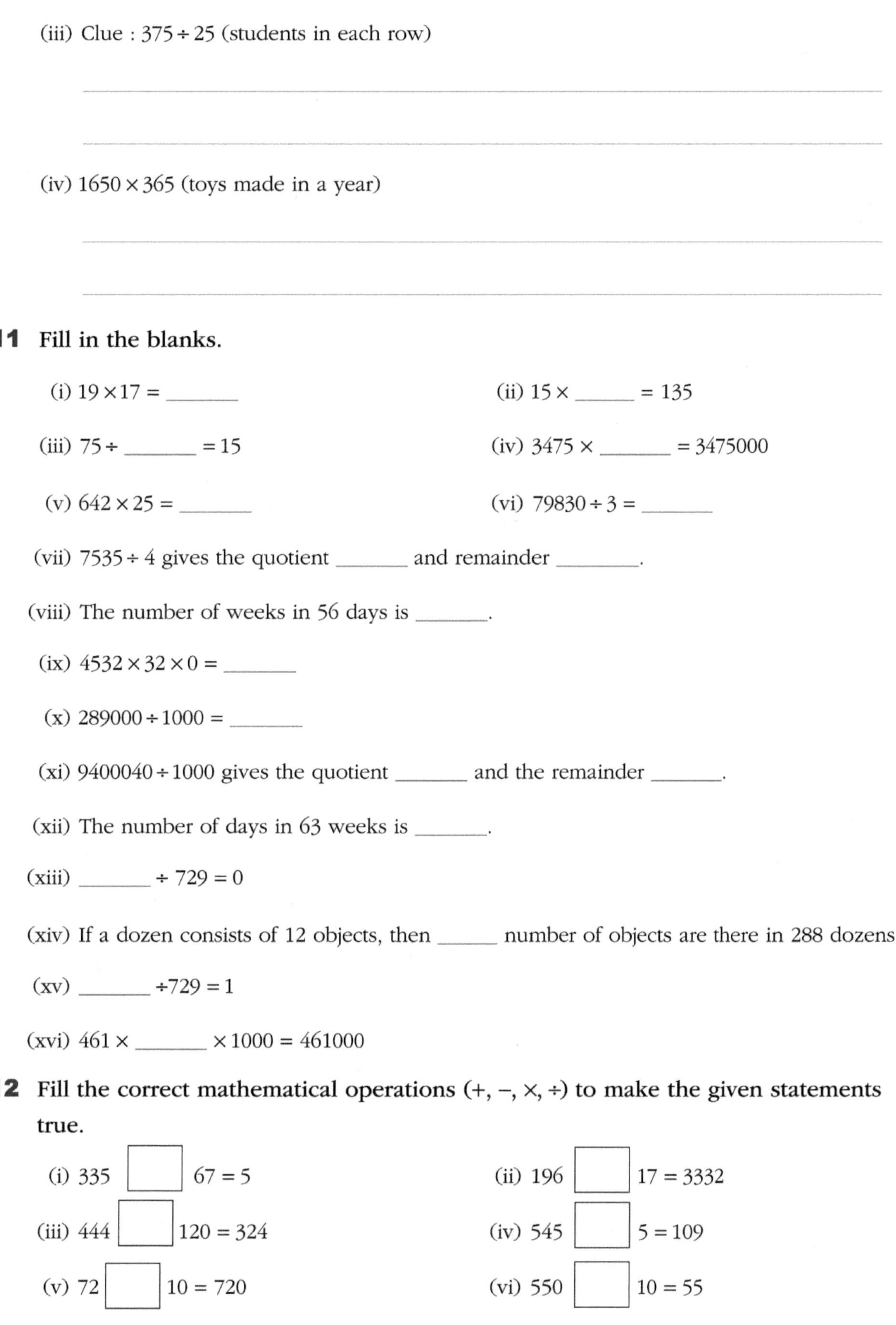

(iii) Clue : $375 \div 25$ (students in each row)

____

____

(iv) 1650×365 (toys made in a year)

____

____

11 Fill in the blanks.

(i) $19 \times 17 =$ _______ (ii) $15 \times$ _______ $= 135$

(iii) $75 \div$ _______ $= 15$ (iv) $3475 \times$ _______ $= 3475000$

(v) $642 \times 25 =$ _______ (vi) $79830 \div 3 =$ _______

(vii) $7535 \div 4$ gives the quotient _______ and remainder _______.

(viii) The number of weeks in 56 days is _______.

(ix) $4532 \times 32 \times 0 =$ _______

(x) $289000 \div 1000 =$ _______

(xi) $9400040 \div 1000$ gives the quotient _______ and the remainder _______.

(xii) The number of days in 63 weeks is _______.

(xiii) _______ $\div 729 = 0$

(xiv) If a dozen consists of 12 objects, then ______ number of objects are there in 288 dozens.

(xv) _______ $\div 729 = 1$

(xvi) $461 \times$ _______ $\times 1000 = 461000$

12 Fill the correct mathematical operations (+, –, ×, ÷) to make the given statements true.

(i) 335 ☐ 67 = 5 (ii) 196 ☐ 17 = 3332

(iii) 444 ☐ 120 = 324 (iv) 545 ☐ 5 = 109

(v) 72 ☐ 10 = 720 (vi) 550 ☐ 10 = 55

13 Fill in the wheels by by dividing/multiplying the numbers in the middle with the number at the centre.

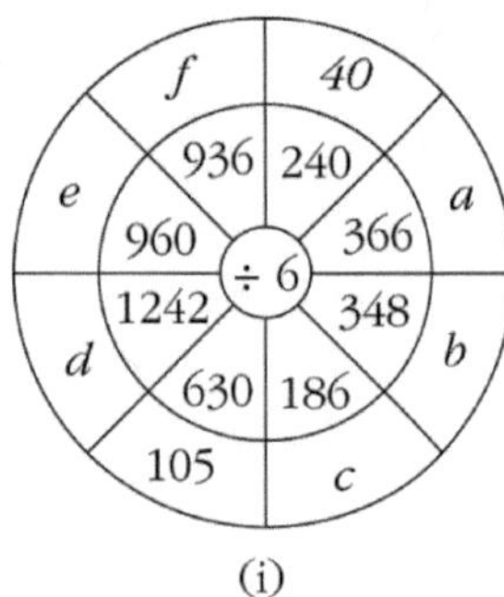

(i)

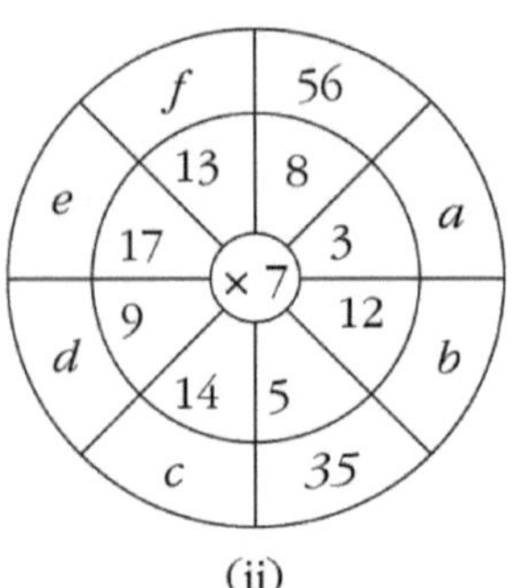

(ii)

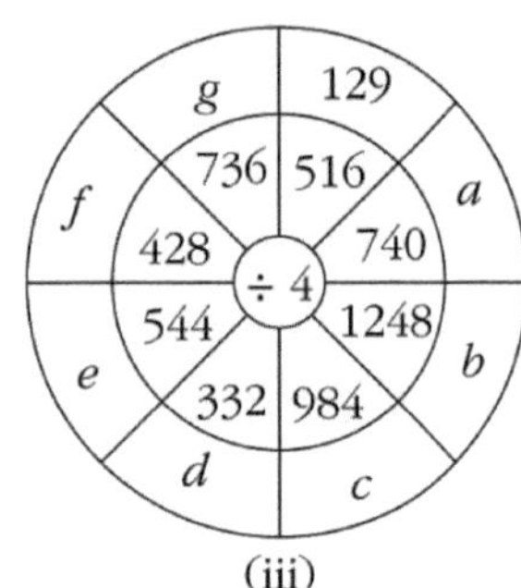

(iii)

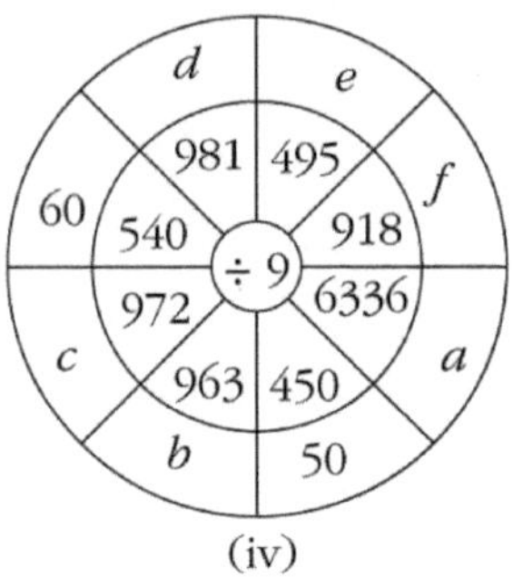

(iv)

14 Choose the correct symbol (>, < or =).

(i) $225 \div 25$ ☐ 4×3 (ii) $600 \div 15$ ☐ 5×6

(iii) 735×3 ☐ $2500 \div 5$ (iv) $(14 \div 7) \times 8$ ☐ $(6 - 2) \times 4$

15 Match the following divisions with their quotient and remainder.

	Quotient		**Division**		**Remainder**
	A		B		C
I.	327	(i)	4229 ÷ 6	(a)	10
II.	28	(ii)	760 ÷ 25	(b)	18
III.	704	(iii)	9876 ÷ 8	(c)	0
IV.	298	(iv)	627 ÷ 21	(d)	4
V.	39	(v)	981 ÷ 3	(e)	15
VI.	1234	(vi)	981 ÷ 25	(f)	5
VII.	350	(vii)	8765 ÷ 25	(g)	1
VIII.	30	(viii)	456 ÷ 16	(h)	6
IX.	242	(ix)	5678 ÷ 19	(i)	8
X.	29	(x)	969 ÷ 4	(j)	16

16 Complete the number tree given below and find the missing number.

(i) 75 → × 3 → *a*; 75 → × 6 → *c*; *a* → × 4 → *b*; *c* → × 2 → *b*; *b* → ÷ 12 → *d*; *d* → × 24 → *e*; *e* → ÷ 8 → *f*

(ii) 56 → × 2 → *a*; 56 → ÷ 7 → *c*; *a* → × 1 → *b*; *c* → × 14 → *b*; *b* → ÷ 4 → *d*; *d* → × 8 → *e*; *e* → × 10 → *f*

17 Word problems.

(i) Raju can write 63 pages of a notebook in one day. How many pages can he write in the month of July?

(ii) Reena works in a company. Her per day salary is ₹ 625. How much money will she earn in a month of 30 days?

(iii) 945 chocolates are to be distributed among 63 students. Find the number of chocolates each student will get.

(iv) Cost of 15 CDs is ₹ 330. Raju wants to buy 45 CDs. How much money should he carry?

(v) A shopkeeper had to pack 23664 eggs. If they were packed in cartons having capacity of 24 eggs, then how many cartons will be needed to pack the eggs?

(vi) 765 juice bottles were sold for ₹ 49725. Mishy bought 46 such juice bottles. How much money did she pay?

(vii) Raman's swimming classes fee is ₹ 3948 for 7 months. If he joins for a year, then how much fee he has to pay?

(viii) Garima has ₹ 500 with her. She wants to buy milk whose cost is ₹ 50 per litre. How many litres of milk can she buy?

(ix) Rishi and Suchi went to a cake shop. Prices of different cakes were written on the board.

Cake	Price per kg
Chocolate	₹ 325
Fruit	₹ 250
Blueberry	₹ 475
Truffle	₹ 375
Chocochip	₹ 400

Rishi bought 3 kg of truffle cake and Suchi bought 5 kg of fruit cake. Who paid more money for the cake and how much?

Chapter 14

How Big? How Heavy?

1 Fill in the blanks.

(i) The amount displaced by any object poured in a liquid is called _______ of the object.

(ii) The volume of a cube having edge 6 cm is _______.

(iii) The volume of a bucket is measured in _______.

(iv) A living room having dimensions of $20 \times 15 \times 10$ has _______ cubic cm of air.

2 Dropping one marble ○ raise the level of water in a beaker by 10 mL.

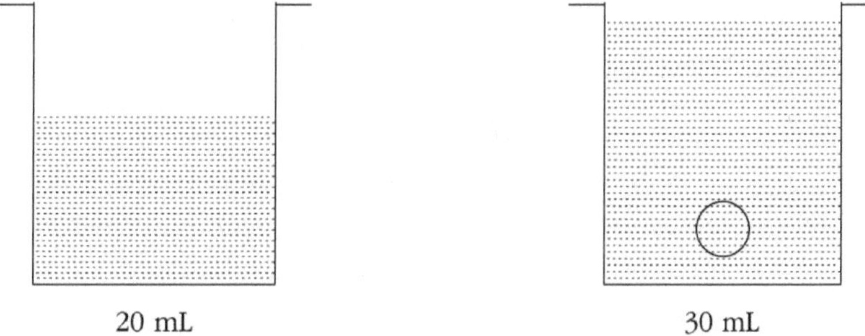

Complete the following table by writing the volume of water raised or number of marbles required to raise the given level of water.

Water raised	Number of marbles
40 mL	4
60 mL	(i) ________
20 mL	(ii) ________
(iii) ________	5
(iv) ________	7

3 If □ has side equal to 2 cm, then find the length of each of the given objects. One has been done for you.

(i) 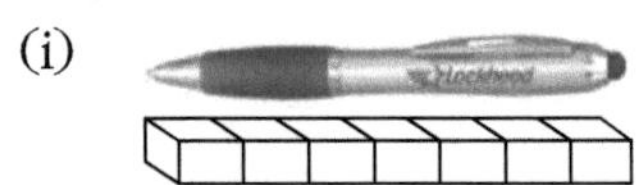

= ____14____ cm

(ii) 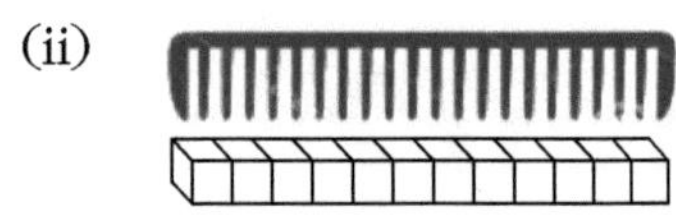

= ________ cm

(iii) 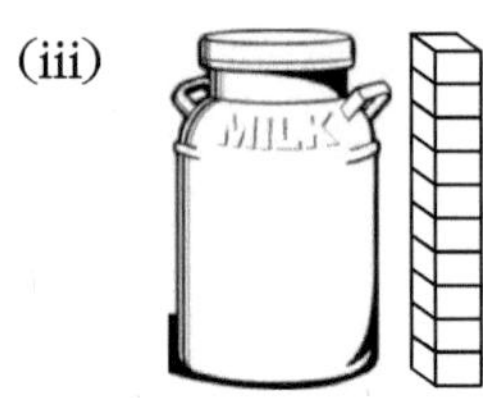

= ________ cm

(iv) 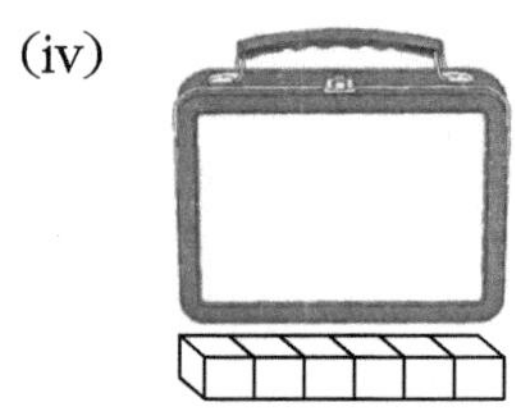

= ________ cm

(v) 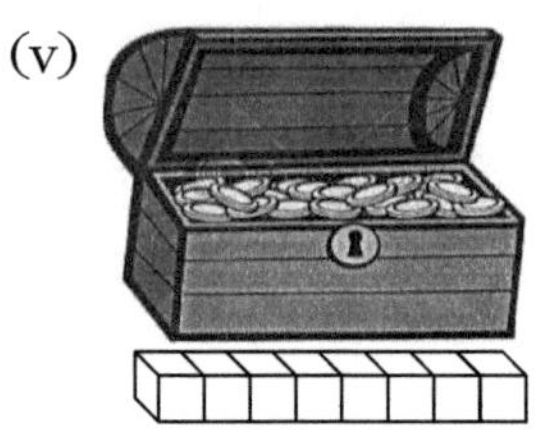

= ________ cm

4 Find the volume of the given figures. One has been done for you

(i) 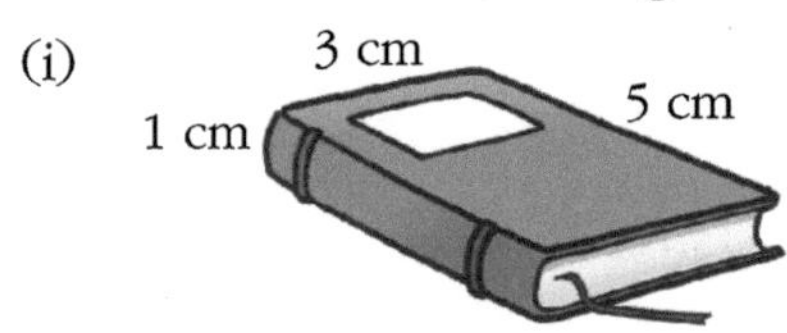

= ____15 cubic cm____

(ii) A book having dimensions 5 cm × 4 cm × 6 cm. = ________

(iii) 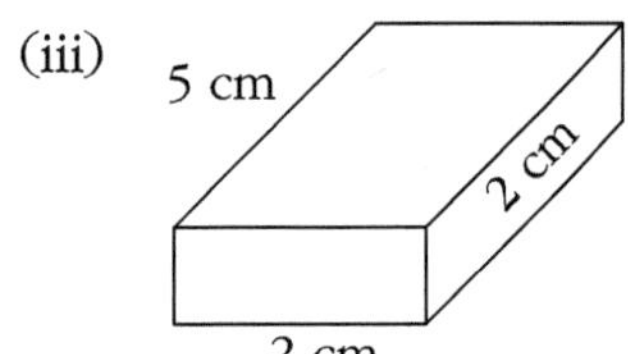

= ________

(iv) 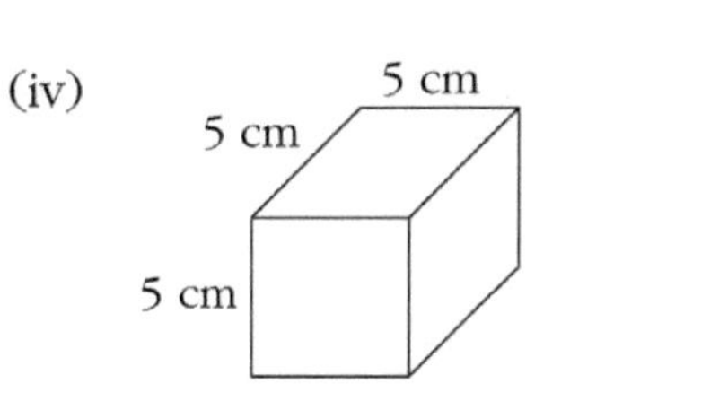

= 

(v) 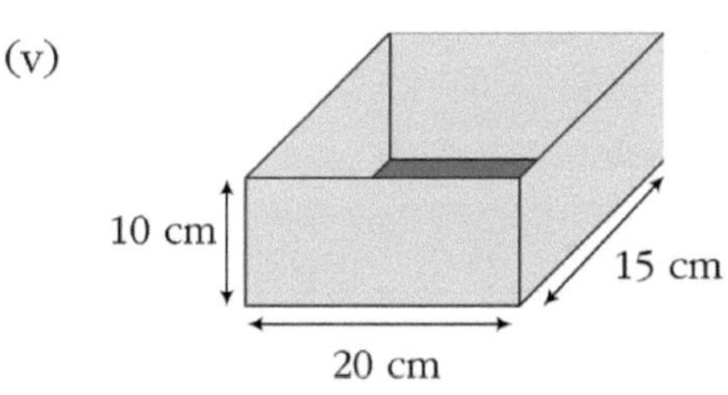

= ______________

(vi) 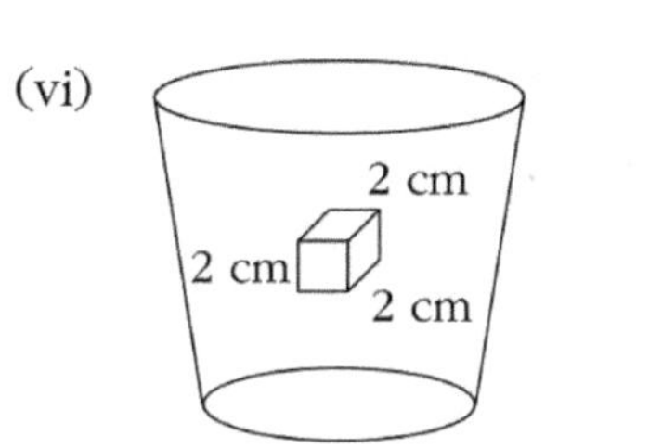

= ______________

5 **Reena is making a bridge using small Tic-Tac boxes. She used the following number of boxes in first layer.**

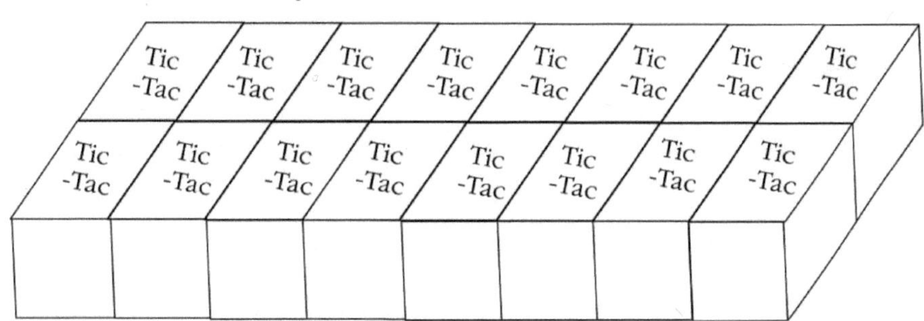

(i) How many Tic-Tac boxes will she use to make 7 such layers?

____

____

(ii) If the volume of one such Tic-Tac box is 8 cubic cm, then find the volume of the bridge having 10 such layers.

____

____

(iii) If the Tic-Tac boxes in 5 layers are now arranged in a line, how many Tic-Tac boxes will be there in the line?

____

____

6 It the weight of one marble (○) is 10 g, then find the weight of the following objects. One has been done for you.

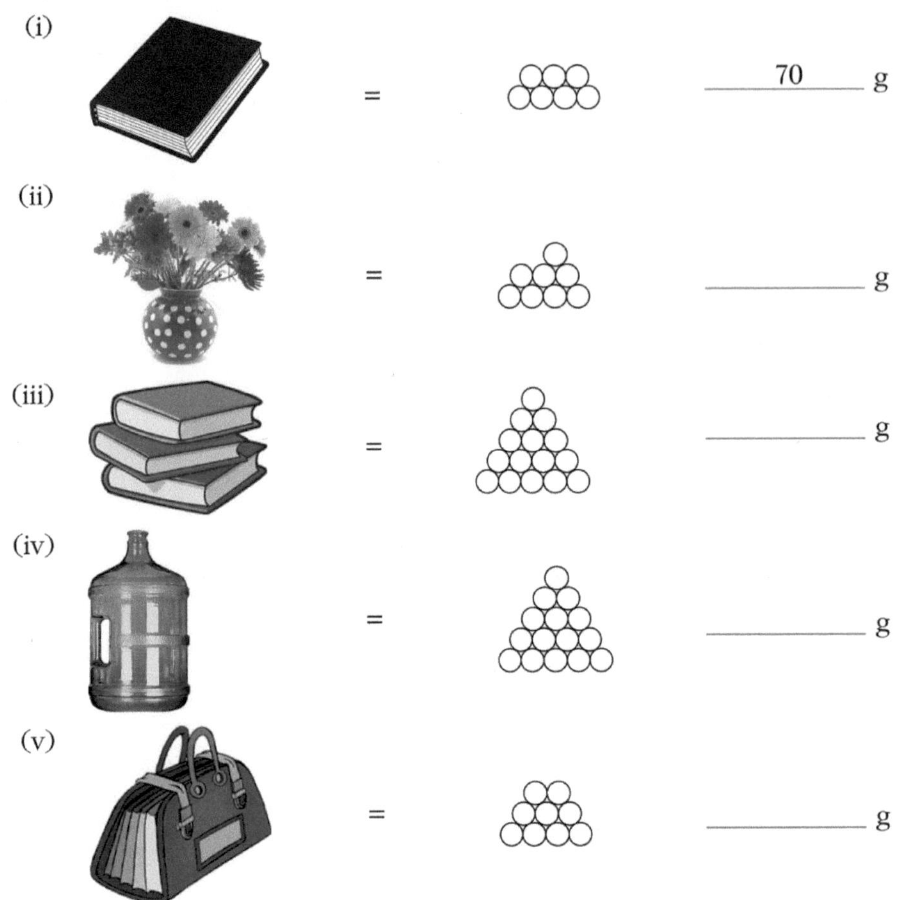

(i) = ○○○○○○○ = 70 g

(ii) = ________ g

(iii) = ________ g

(iv) = ________ g

(v) = ________ g

Which two objects have equal weights?

7 A group of 15 friends are going for trekking for 10 days. They have to pack their bags with things like food, water, etc. The list of food each person will need for one day is given below.

Wheat flour	:	120 g
Rice	:	90 g
Pulses	:	1/5 of the weight of rice and flour
Oil	:	45 g
Sugar	:	65 g
Milk powder	:	45 g
Tea	:	12 g
Porridge	:	50 g for breakfast
Salt	:	6 g
Dried onions	:	12 g
Dried tomatoes	:	10 g

Answer the following questions on the basis of given information.

(i) For 10 days each one will need

(a) _________ g of wheat flour.

(b) _______________ g of rice.

(c) _______________ g of sugar.

(d) _______________ g of milk powder and tea.

(ii) How much dried onions will be required for 10 days for 15 people?

(iii) What is the total weight of food (for 10 days) carried in each bag?

8 **If the weight of a 5 rupees coin is 7 g, then find the weight of a sack containing the following number of coins.**

(i) 700 coins _______________

(ii) 1200 coins _______________

(iii) 1500 coins _______________

(iv) 3560 coins _______________

How many coins are there in the bag whose weight is 39 kg 200 g? _______________

9 If the weight of a 10 rupees coin is 8 g, then find the number of coins in each bag of the given weight.

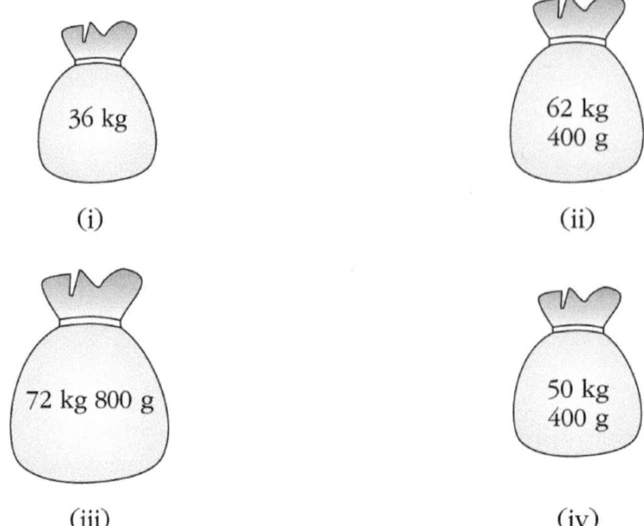

10 Look at the board which is showing the weights of different coins.

₹ 1 coin	3 g
₹ 2 coins	5 g
₹ 5 coins	7 g
₹ 10 coins	8 g

On the basis of above, use the suitable sign to compare the weight of bags in each part.

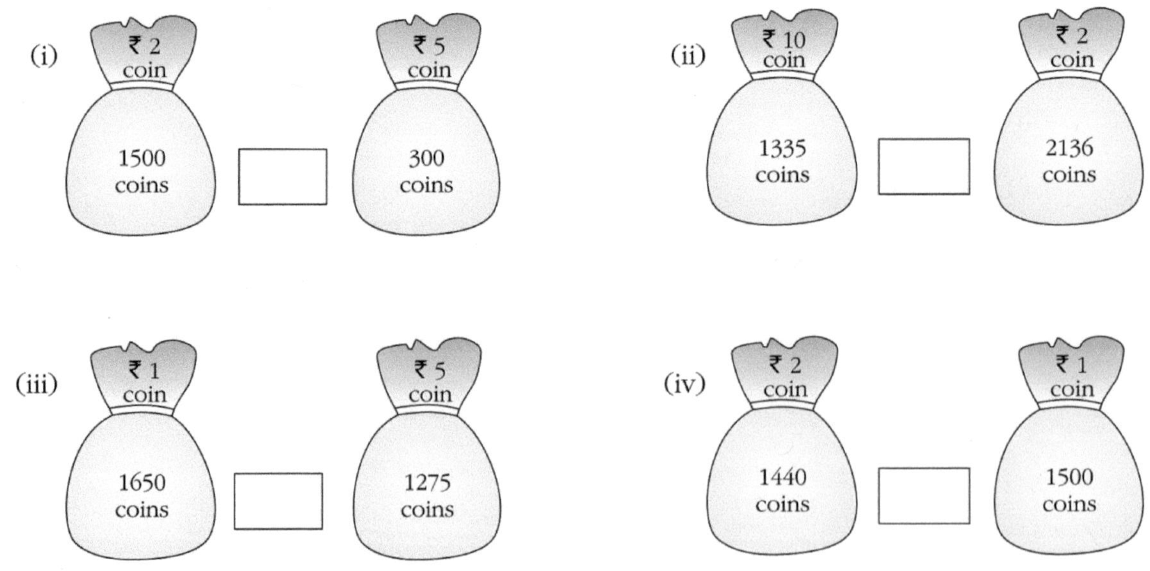

11 State 'True' or 'False.'

(i) Length of [calculator] is measured in kilograms. ☐

(ii) Capacity of milk packet [milk packet] is measured in litres. ☐

(iii) Capacity of small curd pack [yogurt] is measured in grams. ☐

(iv) A bucket [bucket] can store 100 grams of water. ☐

12 Word problems.

(i) The dimensions of a pencil box is 10 cm × 5 cm × 2 cm. Find its volume.

(ii) How many soap cakes of dimensions 10 cm × 8 cm × 6 cm can be packed in a box having dimensions 10 cm × 60 cm × 40 cm?

(iii) How many small boxes of dimensions 2 cm × 1 cm × 3 cm can be packed in a big box of dimensions 12 cm × 10 cm × 18 cm?

(iv) The weight of any object on the moon is 1/6th of the weight on the Earth. An astronaut having weight 72 kg at the Earth went to Moon on a mission. How much does he weigh there?

(v) How many bricks of length 20 cm, breadth 4 cm and height 6 cm will be needed to build a wall of length 10 cm, thickness 6 cm and height 2 m? (1 m = 100 cm)

(vi) Rohan's puppy weighs 3 kg. His friend Rajan got a dog whose weight was 12 times the weight of the puppy. Find the weight of Rajan's dog.

(vii) Sanjeev's cow eat 7 kg of fodder in a day. How many kilograms of fodder will Sanjeev need to feed her cow for a month (30 days)?

Answers

Chapter 1 The Fish Tale

1. (ii) 8 (iii) 7 (iv) 6

2.

	Sum	Estimated sum
(i)	109053	109100
(ii)	89668	89700
(iii)	26486	26500
(iv)	1203	1200
(v)	1279	1300
(vi)	684	700

3.

	Difference	Estimated difference
(ii)	228895	229000
(iii)	61636	62000
(iv)	64785	65000

4. (i) 6 h, 750 (ii) 3000
   (iii) 2850 (iv) 10 h

5. (ii) 1 (iii) 10 lakh
   (iv) 1000 (v) 5
   (vi) 1

6. (i) False (ii) True
   (iii) False (iv) True

7. (i) 10 kg (ii) (a) 1 kg (b) 6 kg
   (iii) 40 kg

8. 2 : 30 am

9. Thursday; 1988

10. ₹ 2390, ₹ 1020

11. 40 students

12. ₹ 70

Chapter 2 Shapes and Angles

1. **Open figures** (ii), (vi)

   Closed figures (i), (iii), (iv), (v)

2. (ii) 4 (iii) 3 (iv) 6
   (v) 5 (vi) 8

3. (i) Obtuse angle (ii) Right angle
   (iii) Acute angle (iv) Obtuse angle

4. (i) - (c), (ii) - (d), (iii) - (b), (iv) - (a)

5. (ii) Acute angle (iii) Obtuse angle
   (iv) Right angle (v) Straight angle
   (vi) Acute angle

6. (i) *'O'*
   (ii) Angle *AOC*, Angle *BOC*
   (iii) Angle *AOE*, Angle *EOD*, Angle *DOB*
   (iv) Angle *COE*, Angle *BOE*, Angle *AOD*, Angle *COD*

7. (i) 4 (ii) 3 (iii) 3
   (iv) 4 (v) 5 (vi) 6

8. (i) Acute angle (ii) Right angle
   (iii) Obtuse angle (iv) Straight angle
   (v) Acute angle (vi) Obtuse angle

10. (i) 120° (ii) 60°
    (iii) 150°

12. (i) 45° (ii) $\frac{1}{3}$
    (iii) 270° (iv) 2

13. A

14. Monu

15. E, F, H, I, L T

Chapter 3 How Many Squares?

1. (ii) 15 cm (iii) 24 cm
   (iv) 20 cm
   (a) (iii) (b) (ii) (c) 4 cm

2. (i) IV, 16 sq cm (ii) I, 2 sq cm
   (iii) 13 sq cm

3. (i) 6 sq cm (ii) 16 sq cm
   (iii) 10 sq cm (iv) 16 sq cm
   (a) (ii) and (iv), 16 (b) 6

4. (i) 7 sq units (ii) 6 sq units
   (iii) 8 sq units (iv) 12 sq units

5. (i) Number of squares = 10, Perimeter = 14 units
   (ii) Number of squares = 7, Perimeter = 14 units
   (iii) Number of squares = 8, Perimeter = 18 units
   (iv) Number of squares = 5, Perimeter = 12 units
   (a) Shape (iii) has the greatest perimeter.

12. (i) D

13. 16 sq units, 8 sq units; Wheat, 8 sq units

Chapter 4 Parts and Wholes

1. (i) (d) (ii) (b)
   (iii) (c) (iv) (a)

2. (ii) $\frac{3}{12}, \frac{9}{12}$ (iii) $\frac{1}{4}, \frac{3}{4}$
   (iv) $\frac{1}{2}, \frac{1}{2}$ (v) $\frac{4}{8}, \frac{4}{8}$

4. (a)

5. (i) Sunflower, $\frac{3}{9}$ (ii) $\frac{2}{9}$
   (iii) $\frac{1}{9}$ (iv) Lily and Rose

6. (i) 6 (ii) 6
   (iii) 12 Apples, 6 Bananas

7. ₹ 300

8. $\frac{1}{2} = \frac{20}{40} = \frac{13}{26} = \frac{12}{24}$

   $\frac{1}{3} = \frac{8}{24}$

   $\frac{2}{3} = \frac{16}{24} = \frac{30}{45} = \frac{24}{36}, \frac{3}{4} = \frac{36}{48} = \frac{27}{36} = \frac{9}{12} = \frac{15}{20}$

   $\frac{2}{5} = \frac{14}{35} = \frac{4}{10} = \frac{22}{55} = \frac{6}{15} = \frac{10}{25} = \frac{20}{50} = \frac{18}{45} = \frac{16}{40}$

9. (i) Yes (ii) Yes
   (iii) No (iv) Yes

10. (i) ₹ 280 (ii) ₹ 84
    (iii) 30 minutes (iv) 10
    (v) $\frac{3}{4}$ kg

11. (i) 25 (ii) 50
    (iii) 80 (iv) 80
    (v) $\frac{5}{6}$ (vi) $\frac{3}{4}$
    (vii) $\frac{1}{6}$ (viii) $\frac{1}{7}$
    (ix) $\frac{3}{10}$

12. (i) ₹ 48 (ii) ₹ 4
    (iii) ₹ 20 (iv) ₹ 45
    (v)

Item	Price (in ₹ per kg)	Amount (in ₹)
Tomato	16	32
Onion	18	63
Brinjal	20	25
Carrot	10	10
Cauliflower	12	6
Potato	8	38
Total		**174**

13. (i) False (ii) True
    (iii) True (iv) True
    (v) False (vi) True
    (vii) False (viii) True

Chapter 5 Does It Look the Same?

1. (ii) 1 (iii) 1
   (iv) 3 (v) 4
   (vi) 2

3. (i) No (ii) Yes
   (iii) Yes (iv) Yes
   (v) Yes (vi) No

4. (ii) No (iii) Yes
   (iv) Yes (v) No (vi) Yes

5. (ii) Yes (iii) Yes
   (iv) No (v) No
   (vi) Yes

6. (ii) ✓ (iii) ✘ (iv) ✓ (v) ✘ (vi) ✓

9. (i) ✓ (ii) ✓ (iii) ✘ (iv) ✘ (v) ✓ (vi) ✓ (vii) ✘ (viii) ✘ (ix) ✘ (x) ✓ (xi) ✓ (xii) ✘ (xiii) ✓ (xiv) ✓ (xv) ✓ (xvi) ✘ (xvii) ✘ (xviii) ✘

Chapter 6 Be My Multiple, I'll be Your Factor

1. (i) 18, 20, 22, 24, 26, 28
(ii) 9, 12, 15, 18, 21, 24, 27
(iii) 18, 24
(iv) Yes

2. FACTOR

3. (i) 6, 9, 12, 15, 18 (ii) 10, 15, 20, 25, 30
(iii) 22, 33, 44, 55, 66 (iv) 28, 42, 56, 70, 84
(v) 36, 54, 72, 90, 108

4. (i) 3, 6, 9, 12, 15, 18, 21, 24, 27, 30, 33, 36, 39, 42, 45, 48
(ii) 4, 8, 12, 16, 20, 24, 28, 32, 36, 40, 44, 48
(iii) 6, 12, 18, 24, 30, 36, 42, 48
(iv) 12, 24, 36, 48

5. (ii) (a) 60 (b) 15
(iii) (a) 15 (b) 105 (c) 35
(iv) (a) 12 (b) 36 (c) 18 (d) 36

6. (i) 6, 12, 18 (ii) 15, 30, 45
(iii) 35, 70, 105

7. (i) 24 (ii) 48 (iii) 150 (iv) 36

8.

	Factors	Number of factors
(i)	1, 2, 4, 8	4
(ii)	1, 2, 3, 4, 6, 12	6
(iii)	1, 3, 5, 15	4
(iv)	1, 2, 4, 5, 10, 20	6
(v)	1, 17	2
(vi)	1, 19	2

9. (i) 2 (ii) 2, 3, 6
(iii) 5 (iv) 2, 4, 8
(v) 2, 5, 10 (vi) 3, 5, 15

11. (ii) (a) 4
(iii) (a) 5 (b) 11
(iv) (a) 3 (b) 7 (c) 5
(v) (a) 13 (b) 3 (c) 11

12. (i) 6 (ii) 6
(iii) 8 (iv) 15
(v) 30 (vi) 3

13.
(i)

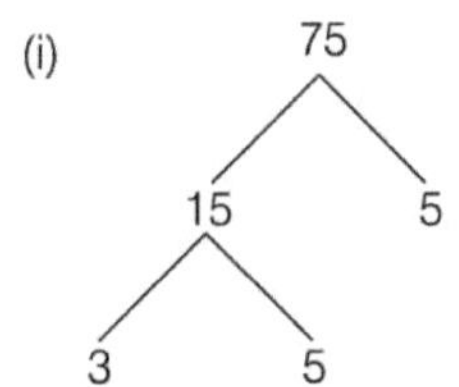

(ii)
- 60
  - 12
    - 2
    - 6
      - 2
      - 3
  - 5

(iii)
- 63
  - 9
    - 3
    - 3
  - 7

(iv)
- 225
  - 45
    - 5
    - 9
      - 3
      - 3
  - 5

(v)
- 320
  - 64
    - 32
      - 2
      - 16
        - 2
        - 8
          - 2
          - 4
            - 2
            - 2
    - 2
  - 5

14. (i) True (ii) False
(iii) True
(iv) True
(v) False
(vi) True

15. (i) 120 (ii) 144 L
(iii) 140 (iv) 60
(v) 121 (vi) 60 ft

Chapter 7 Can You See the Pattern?

2. 8 Steps

3. (i) (a) (ii) (b)
(iii) (b) (iv) (a)

4. (i) (f) (ii) (e)
(iii) (d) (iv) (b)
(v) (c)

5. (i)

11	**7**	3
4	9	**8**
6	**5**	10

(ii)

13	**6**	11
9	**14**	7
8	10	**12**

6. (i) 84 (ii) 40
(iii) 48 (iv) 15
(v) 90

7. (i) (a) 7 (b) 4
(ii) (a) 20 (b) 27
(c) 11 (d) 77
(e) 63 (f) 9

8. (ii) 26, 34 (iii) 300, 600, 400
(iv) 145, 120, 600

10. (i) 324, 486, 648 (ii) 8889, 88889

11. (i) 12 (ii) 20

12. (i) 15 (ii) 25
(iii) 29 (iv) 49

13. (i) (a) 12321 (b) 1111, 1111
(ii) (a) 1234, 4 (b) 98765, 5
(iii) (a) $1+3+5+7+9+11+13$
(b) 10×10

Chapter 8 Mapping Your Way

1. (i) 90° (ii) Acute angle
(iii) Quadrilateral

2. (i) 32 km (ii) East

3. (i) Arihant–Rajghat–DU (ii) Arihant

5. (i) 120 km
(ii) (d)
(iii) Bodhgaya and Murgen
(iv) South
(v) 100 km
(vi) 100 km

6. (i) 24 sq cm (ii) 3 times
(iii) (a) (iv) 5 times

Chapter 9 Boxes and Sketches

1. 2-D shapes (i), (iv), (vi), (vii)
3-D shapes (ii), (vi), (v)

3. (i), (iii), (iv)

4. (i)

5. (i)-(c), (ii)-(d),
(iii)-(b), (iv)-(a)

6. (iii)

7. (ii)

10. (i)-(d), (ii)-(a),
(iii)-(b), (iv)-(c)

11. Top view Side view Front view

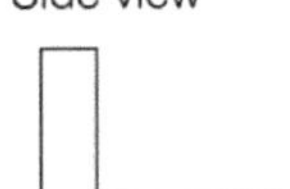

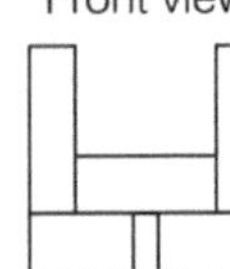

12. (i) 14
(ii) 90

13. (i) False
(ii) True
(iii) False

Chapter 10 Tenths and Hundredths

1. (ii) 8.3 cm (iii) 6.7 cm
   (iv) 7.6 cm (v) 10.3 cm
2. (ii) 11, 7 (iii) 9, 1
   (iv) 10, 4 (v) 6, 5
3. (ii) 0.45 (iii) 5.32 (iv) 6.001
   (v) 0.57 (vi) 32.3 (vii) 46.55
4. (i) 25.3 (ii) 325 (iii) 3.2 (iv) 0.46
   (v) 76 (vi) 0.7325 (vii) 6375
5. (i)-(e), (ii)-(b), (iii)-(d),
   (iv)-(c), (v)-(a)
6. (i) > (ii) = (iii) >
   (iv) >
7. (i) 2.5 cm (ii) 0.25 m
   (iii) ₹ 2.52 (iv) ₹ 25.50
   (v) 7.2 m (vi) 25 cm
   (vii) 840 paise
8. (ii) 0.41 (iii) 0.05 (iv) 0.4
9. (ii)-III (a), (iii)-I (b),
   (iv)-VI (f), (v)-II (c),
   (vi)-IV (e)
10. (i) 1.35 (ii) 26.4
    (iii) 202.13 (iv) 56
    (v) 75.6 (vi) 2.05
11. (i) ₹ 10.25 (ii) ₹ 21 (iii) Sonia
    (iv) 1.35 m; 2.25 m (v) ₹ 12.25
    (vi) 40.2°C
12. (i) 65.5 (ii) 15.79
    (iii) 87.28
13. (i) Japan (ii) Ruchi's friend; ₹ 3949
    (iii) ₹ 974 (iv) 500
14. (i) Srinagar (ii) 47.2 mm
    (iii) 4.7 mm (iv) 16.9 mm
15. (i) Gold (ii) 2700.42°C
    (iii) Water (iv) 2743.69°C

Chapter 11 Area and its Boundary

1. I. (i) 315, 72 (ii) 270, 66
   II. (i) 30 (ii) 21 (iii) 72
2. (i) 14 m (ii) 12 cm, 9 sq cm
   (iii) 25 m (iv) 64 m, 240 sq m
   (v) 36 cm, 80 sq cm (vi) 11 cm, 121 sq cm
4. (i) 49 sq cm (ii) 96 sq cm
   (iii) 28 cm (iv) 44 cm
   (iv) 47 sq cm (vi) 16 cm
5. (i) 12 cm, 8 sq cm (ii) 10 cm, 5 sq cm
   (iii) 14 cm, 8 sq cm (iv) 20 cm, 14 sq cm
6. (i) 15 cm (ii) 13 cm
   (iii) 20 cm (iv) 18 cm (v) 25 cm
7. (i) (b) (ii) (b) (iii) (a) (iv) (d)
8. (i) 36 cm (ii) 144
   (iii) 14 m
   (iv) (a) 34 sq cm (b) 40 sq cm
   (v) 17680 sq cm (vi) 2500 sq m
9. I. (i) 200 (ii) 340
   (iii) 3202 (iv) 32000.2
   II. (iv)
10. 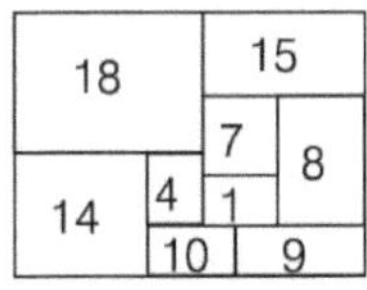

Perimeter = 130 cm
Area = 1056 sq cm

Chapter 12 Smart Charts

1. (i) (b) 17 (c) 14 (d) 8 (e) 23
   (f) 15
   (ii) 95 (iii) Litchi, 23 (iv) False (v) Guava
   (vi) 10
3. 8
4. (i) Luge = 14, Bobsledding = 4, Ski jumping = 12
   (ii) (a) Bobsledding (b) Luge (c) 10
5. (i) Ben 10 (ii) Doremon
   (iii) Spiderman (iv) Tom & Jerry
6. (i) Deer = 240, Tiger = 180, Chimpanzee = 270, Lion = 180, Elephant = 120, Giraffe = 90
   (ii) True (iii) Tiger and Lion (iv) 60
8. (i) (c) (ii) (c) (iii) 7th year
9. (i) 12 (ii) 14
10. (i) 40 min (ii) Saturday and Sunday
    (iii) True

Chapter 13 Ways to Multiply and Divide

1. (i) 672 (ii) 1404 (iii) 2052 (iv) 1512

2. (ii) 8416, 8400 (iii) 11102, 11100
(iv) 21648, 21600

3. (i) 112, 216, 120 (ii) ₹ 42760

4. (i) ₹ 1200 (ii) Yes (iii) ₹ 14400

5. (i) ₹ 6222 (ii) ₹11700 (iii) ₹ 7360

6. $b = 2, c = 3$

7. (i) 1191 (ii) 1315 (iii) 322 (iv) 801
(v) 1440 (vi) 352 (vii) 289 (viii) 456

9. (ii) (c) (iii) (b) (iv) (c)

11. (i) 323 (ii) 9 (iii) 5
(iv) 1000 (v) 16050 (vi) 26610
(vii) 1883, 3 (viii) 8 (ix) 0
(x) 289 (xi) 9400, 40 (xii) 441
(xiii) 0 (xiv) 3456 (xv) 729
(xvi) 1

12. (i) ÷ (ii) ×
(iii) – (iv) ÷
(v) × (vi) ÷

13. (i) (a) 61 (b) 58 (c) 31
(d) 207 (e) 160 (f) 156
(ii) (a) 21 (b) 84 (c) 98
(d) 63 (e) 119 (f) 91
(iii) (a) 185 (b) 312 (c) 246
(d) 83 (e) 136 (f) 107
(g) 184
(iv) (a) 704 (b) 107 (c) 108
(d) 109 (e) 55 (f) 102

14. (i) < (ii) > (iii) > (iv) =

15. I.–(v)-(c) II.–(viii)-(i)
III.–(i)-(f) IV.–(ix)-(j)
V.–(vi)-(h) VI.–(iii)-(d)
VII.–(vii)-(e) VIII.–(ii)-(a)
IX.–(x)-(g) X.–(iv)-(b)

16. (i) (a) 225 (b) 900 (c) 450 (d) 75
(e) 1800 (f) 225
(ii) (a) 112 (b) 112 (c) 8 (d) 28
(e) 224 (f) 2240

17. (i) 1953 (ii) ₹ 18750
(iii) 15 (iv) ₹ 990
(v) 986 (vi) ₹ 2990
(vii) ₹ 6768 (viii) 10 litres
(ix) Suchi, ₹ 125

Chapter 14 How Big? How Heavy?

1. (i) volume (ii) 216 cubic cm
(iii) litre (iv) 3000

2. (i) 6 (ii) 2
(iii) 50 mL (iv) 70 mL

3. (ii) 24 (iii) 20
(iv) 12 (v) 16

4. (ii) 120 cubic cm (iii) 20 cubic cm
(iv) 125 cubic cm (v) 3000 cubic cm
(vi) 8 cubic cm

5. (i) 112
(ii) 1280 cubic cm
(iii) 80

6. (ii) 80 (iii) 150
(iv) 150 (v) 90
Books and a tumbler

7. (i) (a) 1200 (b) 900
(c) 650 (d) 570
(ii) 1800 g (iii) 4970 g

8. (i) 4900 g (ii) 8400 g
(iii) 10500 g (iv) 24920 g
5600

9. (i) 4500 (ii) 7800
(iii) 9100 (iv) 6300

10. (i) > (ii) = (iii) < (iv) >

11. (i) False (ii) True
(iii) True (iv) False

12. (i) 100 cubic cm (ii) 50
(iii) 360 (iv) 12 kg
(v) 25 (vi) 36 kg
(vii) 210 kg

Printed by Libri Plureos GmbH in Hamburg,
Germany